W9-BKA-908

THE THESES WERE NOT POSTED

The Theses Were Not Posted

LUTHER BETWEEN REFORM AND REFORMATION

by Erwin Iserloh

INTRODUCTION BY
MARTIN E. MARTY

BEACON PRESS : BOSTON

Translated from the
second edition (1967) of
*Luther zwischen Reform
und Reformation* by
Erwin Iserloh

Footnotes have been
condensed and adapted
for the English edition
by the translator

Originally published in Germany
by Verlag Aschendorff, Münster
as Volume 23/24 of the series
*Katholisches Leben und Kämpfen
im Zeitalter der Glaubensspaltung*

Library of Congress catalog card number: 68-14706

Published simultaneously in Canada
by Saunders of Toronto, Ltd.

Beacon Press books are published under the auspices of
the Unitarian Universalist Association

Printed in the United States of America

FOR JOSEPH LORTZ

WITH DEEP RESPECT AND GRATITUDE

INTRODUCTION

ON ALL HALLOWS' EVE in 1517 an intense young German monk strode through a crowd, hammer in hand. With all eyes upon him he tacked a long parchment to the door of the Wittenberg castle church. He posted ninety-five theses for debate which concerned the Catholic system of penance as it related to grace. The crowd, gathered to celebrate All Saints' Day and to view the church's thousands of holy relics, read the theses. A sense of shock, surprise, and delight was apparent; soon the people dispersed, to begin spreading word of the theses across Europe. Before many seasons passed, empires tumbled, popes were threatened, European Christendom was divided, the world was changed. The scene, since repeated in thousands of Reformation Day pageants, is wonderfully dramatic, but . . .

It never happened.

So argues Erwin Iserloh, a Roman Catholic historian and theologian from Münster, Germany. In this book he tries to destroy one of those cherished primal images which have been stamped on the minds of moderns. Iserloh has no negativistic interest; here is neither muckraking nor sensationalism for its own sake. Nor does his Catholicism move him to vicious attacks on the arch-heretic monk Martin Luther. Had the pope responded to the urging of many people in the 450th year of the Reformation, he would have withdrawn the ban of excommunication against Luther. Iserloh, as this book makes clear, could have cheered such a move. Yet, at first glance, the book seems to be destructive.

No hammer, no crowd scene, no posting, no instant public

appeal or response—with these missing, what is left of Reformation Day and how does one begin to mark and characterize the beginnings of Protestantism? Iserloh tells what is left: Luther performed a sixteenth-century version of going to the post office; he mailed a letter to a bishop and made known to the scholarly world that he would like to question the commercialization of the treasures of the church, as typified in the selling of indulgences by a Dominican, Johannes Tetzel.

The picture that Iserloh tries to shatter has been part of popular imagination and scholarly lore since at least 1546 when Luther's colleague and intimate, Philipp Melanchthon, calmly reported the incident. Not until the late 1950s did German scholars—they always have to tamper with everything!—begin to question the Melanchthon story. Hans Volz, an editor of the prestigious Weimar edition of Luther's works, began the stir by dating the posting a day after October 31. But it was Iserloh who inaugurated the noisier debate by arguing that there never had been a posting. (Another Catholic, Klemens Honselmann of Paderborn, also says that there was no posting and argues that the theses did not even become known until mid-December, a month later than Iserloh dates the public commotion.)

The evidence for the traditionalist and revisionist positions is slim but tantalizing. Melanchthon was not on the scene in 1517 and did not bother to tell the story until almost three decades later, after Luther's death. Is he a credible witness in this case? Iserloh says that if we follow Melanchthon, as the traditionalists do, we make Luther out to be a liar, for Luther in his reports on the beginnings of reform insisted that he had not made the theses public. How the leading Protestant defender of the tradition, Kurt Aland, also of Münster, answers Iserloh and defends Luther's veracity will be unfolded on the following pages; there is no point in giving away the details of a fascinating detective story or a German scholarly debate! More important for the moment is the question: Does any of this matter?

Historians have no problem answering that the story has intrinsic worth. People should want to read it for its own sake, the way they read detective stories. What is more, if one can demonstrate the falsity of reporting one of the great episodes of world history, he should do so. The ethics of the historian's profession is at stake, and the public should care. The big lie is built upon carelessness about little falsehoods, including accidental ones; if historians do not care about accuracy and truth, who will?

The issue reaches the public at a somewhat different point. People act on the basis of images, remembered pictures, gestures which portray the style of persons and movements. Did Napoleon take the crown of empire from the pope and crown himself in 1804, or did the two have a prearrangement? Did William Penn ever sign a treaty with the Indians, as the Benjamin West painting on a thousand classroom walls suggests? (There is no evidence that he did.) Did Washington kneel to pray at Valley Forge, as the postage stamp and a window in the Capitol have it? There is no foundation in fact for such an incident or posture. But the public makes up its mind about the Napoleons and Penns and Washingtons on the basis of such images. Luther's style and the popular recall of the Reformation are closely related to the gestures of October 31.

Seen in that light, Iserloh's case takes on more importance. He is dealing with an issue which helps explain the divided mind of the modern world and the spiritual malaise of the West. There are not many such incidents. In the first century Christians and Jews began to go their separate ways; in the eleventh century after long ages of tension Christians of East and West divided; in the sixteenth century western Christians split and went separate ways. How, when, and under what circumstances these schisms occurred are important questions especially when people seek reunion and healing as they do today.

One group of people looks at Luther, the "obedient rebel," the Catholic Protestant, as a conservative and careful reformer who wanted to stay in continuity with the Catholic church of the past. They will find support in Iserloh, for he shows Luther to be a responsible academic scholar whose conscience caused him to react to abuses and untruths but whose manner of reaction prevented him from breaking the accepted rules of the game.

The other group looks at Luther as a radical and revolutionary Protestant who wanted to stress the difference between his gospel and the church he had known. Those who look for this sometimes heroic and sometimes demagogic Luther will prefer the dramatic story of the hammer and the crowds.

Whether or not Iserloh converts anybody new with his narrative, everyone will find new light thrown on the image of the obedient rebel. When families try to patch up their squabbles, as western Christians are trying to do today, they find it important to learn all they can about why a favorite son left home or was thrown out. Did he, to change the picture, shout "Fire!" in a crowded theatre or did he push the alarm behind the scenes?

The context of Luther's dissemination of the theses illumines the whole scene of debate in his time. In his case, at least, the medium had much to do with the message. He did write theses for debate; he did offer them; they became public matters. This much is certain. Whether he did it on October 31, or a day later; whether they became known instantly on the church door or in mid-November or mid-December,—these are issues for prissy and petty German scholars to ponder. But viewed from another angle, the what and the how of his acts are united.

Take a modern parallel. It makes a difference whether Stokely Carmichael, Floyd McKissick, or H. Rap Brown argue black power before a crowd in a burning Detroit or in a letter to the Center for the Study of Democratic Institutions. It makes a difference whether Charles de Gaulle shouts for a free Quebec in a Montreal mob scene or in letters of negotiation with Canadian officials. So it matters whether Luther wanted to throw a spark in the German tinder—the mood against Rome was angry and German nationalism and the impulse for church reform were growing—or whether he wanted to follow accepted channels.

German scholarship being what it is, this book has not been permitted to sweep the crowded field. Kurt Aland in particular has viewed the same evidence and come up with some support for the traditional view. Here is a classic case in historical studies: we await more evidence but in the meantime we can play serious games with a few documents, judging them in part in the light of our assumptions about various actors and movements in history. The case is certainly not closed with the publication of this book.

Whether closed or open as a case, as a book this study will do more than appeal to readers of intellectual detective stories. For one thing, it will give newcomers to theological debate a mental workout; too much so, for my taste, on the opening pages. My advice: skip the first pages (to p. 13) where Iserloh defines indulgence controversies with an overdose of technical Latin. Come back to them after you are well into the plot, which really begins when the German economic situation is introduced. By that time you will care more about the definitions. But we need better reasons than mental gymnastics, in any case.

Try another: Iserloh by his approach calls attention to the current well mannered state of Protestant–Catholic scholarship. The debates are intense, but they do not follow confessional lines. Both sides number Protestant and Catholic advocates. Iserloh admits that much of what Luther saw to be wrong in the church of his day was wrong and that many of today's problems derive from ills of that day. He comes on strong as the defender of Luther's honesty and integrity. Such fairness on the part of Catholics is not rare today, but more readers will become aware of it through access to this document.

The book serves in another way. It calls a new generation's

attention to the desperate urgency with which people then debated issues of heaven, hell, and purgatory. (A sour Jacques Maritain complains in *Le paysan de la Garonne*, "There are three things that an intelligent priest must on no account preach about today: the hereafter, the cross, and sanctity.") Sin and grace, the destiny of the individual soul, the traffic in indulgences, the experience of terror or forgiveness—these were of cultural significance in the sixteenth century as black power and white backlash, poverty and abundance, questions of absurdity and meaninglessness are today.

In stressing their importance, Iserloh also demonstrates how far we are from the men and issues of the sixteenth century. Today "the problem of God" replaces their "the problem of a gracious God." Today the church bells still ring, but they seem to meet no response from the skies as they did to the Europeans of 1517. Today people experience apathy or dread more than they fear "the devils on the rooftops" of that earlier day. But those who deal with the heirs of Catholic–Protestant Europe will never understand or serve them well until they can get back to the frame of mind of people who let the northwest European family quarrel dominate the spiritual story of subsequent centuries. "Thus Luther's life receives its meaning from the fact that it connects all the concrete events in which the new religiousness was embraced and established." (Wilhelm Dilthey). The style of Luther's most remembered acts relates to that new religiousness which has become integral to our culture.

New Left historians today are in search of a usable past, looking for radical precedents in western history. Some of them are returning to the young Luther. The college generation, nurtured on the psychoanalytic studies of Norman O. Brown, Erik Erikson, and playwright John Osborne, identifies more readily with the shook-up Luther than it ever could have with the old Germanic culture-hero our fathers remembered. The ecumenical movement restudies Luther as the archetypal obedient rebel. The Protestant churches are just recovering from celebrating the 450 years since Luther's ninety-five theses. Such a moment seems to be a good time for drawing the attention of a new public to the endless debate about the beginnings, the character, the quality, and the style of early reform.

Erwin Iserloh's book is a probe, a provocation. He does not call today's generation to go back to Luther as the *homo religiosus*, the religious man to whom theological matters were so urgent that he handled them with dreadful care, saving himself for moments of creative recklessness. No, the author is content only to set him before us in a fragment of new light, in the hope that more will be brought to understand the past before they act to help shape the future.

Martin E. Marty
The University of Chicago

CONTENTS

ABBREVIATIONS

W *D. Martin Luthers Werke, Kritische Gesamtausgabe* (Weimar: 1883–). References give volume, page, and line number.

WBr *D. Martin Luthers Werke, Kritische Gesamtausgabe, Briefwechsel* (Weimar: 1930–). References give volume and page number followed by the line number within the letter referred to.

WTr *D. Martin Luthers Werke, Kritische Gesamtausgabe, Tischreden* (Weimar: 1912–). References give volume and page number followed by the number of the recorded table remark.

LW *Luther's Works—The American Edition*, published in fifty-five volumes by Concordia Publishing House of St. Louis and Fortress Press of Philadelphia, 1955–. References give volume and page number, with the name of the translator following in parentheses.

DS H. Denziger and A. Schönmetzer, *Enchiridion Symbolorum*, 33rd ed. (Barcelona: 1965).

PREFACE

THIS MONOGRAPH should have appeared four years ago. One reason for the delay was the continuing discussion about the historicity of Luther's public posting of the ninety-five theses on indulgences on October 31, 1517. The discussion appears now to have reached a pause and the results can be taken into account all through this book.

At the end of such a discussion, it is hard to mark off precisely what one has received from others from that which one himself has contributed. Thus I am grateful to all who have taken part in the discussion. First, I wish to express my gratitude to Professor Konrad Repgen, for if I remember rightly it was he who first expressed the suspicion that the posting of the theses might well be a legend, and that without it the events of October 31, 1517, would be much easier to understand. I am especially indebted to the work of my discussion partners, Hans Volz, Kurt Aland, and Klemens Honselmann who kindly allowed me to read the page proofs of his book on the original composition and the earliest printings of Luther's indulgence theses. Actually, my study does not bring new and unknown material to light, but it is based on the most recent Reformation research. Also, my own assistants in the Catholic Ecumenical Institute of the University in Münster, Vinzenz Pfnür, Wolfdieter Theurer, and Jared Wicks, have given me valued help.

The discussion of the past four years was at times marked by sharp exchanges, but happily never by interconfessional polemics. Someone remarked approvingly that he could hardly tell whether it was the Protestant or the Catholic participants who showed the greater sympathy for Luther. However that may be, Luther's own words in *De Servo Arbitrio* should guide us: "Amicus Plato, amicus Socrates, sed praehonoranda veritas." (W 18, 610, 10f.)

Erwin Iserloh
Münster, October 1967

THE THESES WERE NOT POSTED

I. INDULGENCES IN DOCTRINE AND HISTORY

AN INDULGENCE is a remission of temporal punishment due for sin, which is granted by the church and is valid before God. However, there is no comprehensive binding declaration on indulgences from the magisterium of the church. The Council of Trent made its response to the Reformation attack on indulgences in this quite general assertion: first, that the church has received the power from Christ to grant indulgences; and secondly, that for Christians the gaining of indulgences is very salutary.[1] The "treasury of the church" as the basis of indulgences was first mentioned by the magisterium in a document signed by Clement VI in 1343.[2] The document also states that a genuine spirit of penance is a prerequisite for gaining an indulgence. Contemporary canon law describes an indulgence thus: ". . . a remission before God of temporal punishment due for sins after the guilt of the sins has been removed. Ecclesiastical

[1] "Since the power of granting indulgences was conferred by Christ on the Church, and she has made use of such power divinely given to her (cf. Matt. 16:19; 18:18) even in the earliest times, the holy synod teaches and commands that the use of indulgences, most salutary to a Christian people and approved by the authority of the sacred councils, is to be retained in the Church." From H. Denzinger, *The Sources of Catholic Dogma*, translated by Roy J. Deferrari (St. Louis: 1957), n. 989 (Denzinger-Schönmetzer, *Enchiridion Symbolorum* [Barcelona: 1963], n. 1835). The council, however, urged that moderation be observed in granting indulgences, so that too great leniency would not sap the spirit of penance in the church. The abuses that had given indulgences a bad name were to be abolished, above all by removing any occasion for avarice. For all practical purposes, indulgences for money have disappeared.

[2] Denzinger-Schönmetzer, *Enchiridion Symbolorum*, n. 1025ff.

authority grants this remission out of the treasury of the church, in the form of an absolution (*per modum absolutionis*) for the living and in the form of intercession (*per modum suffragii*) for the departed."[3] These declarations leave open important points of both history and theology regarding indulgences, e.g., the precise meaning of *per modum absolutionis* and *per modum suffragii*, and the nature of temporal punishment for sin.

On November 9, 1965, the fathers of the Second Vatican Council were given a document — "*positio*" — concerning the renewal of the indulgence system and were asked to express their minds on the topic.[4] The document sought to shift the emphasis regarding indulgences away from quantitative thinking and to stress the qualitative elements. The ensuing discussion brought out a basic agreement that the church can by intercession aid the penitential efforts of the faithful and thereby gain from God the remission of temporal punishment due for sin. But at the same time any mathematical computation of this aid is wholly out of place. Patriarch Maximos IV Saigh stressed that indulgences are a relatively late development in the church, arising in the West in the Middle Ages and remaining unknown in the eastern churches. Bernard Cardinal Alfrink urged that an indulgence must not be considered as the remission of purely vindictive punishments, but as part of the total process of a Christian's renewal and purification. Franziskus Cardinal König stressed that the practical difficulties with indulgences stem from the traditional theology of indulgences which thought too materialistically of the treasury of the church and which arbitrarily distinguished between jurisdictional absolution and intercessory prayer.

[3] "Omnes magni faciant indulgentias seu remissionem coram Deo poenae temporalis debitae pro peccatis, ad culpam quod attinet iam deletis, quam ecclesiastica auctoritas ex thesauro Ecclesiae concedit pro vivis per modum absolutionis, pro defunctis per modum suffragii." *Codex iuris canonici*, canon 911.

[4] The following statements on indulgences at Vatican II are taken from the sourcebook by L. A. Dorn and W. Seibel, *Tagebuch des Konzils, Die Arbeit der vierten Session* (Nürnberg-Eichstätt: 1966), pp. 233f. and 243–51.

Julian Cardinal Döpfner said that we must take account of the thirteenth-century shift in thought on indulgences from the level of sign (ecclesiastical penance) to the thing itself (remission by God of temporal punishment). For a freely accepted, ecclesial, satisfactory penance is a quasi-sacramental sign of the unseen temporal punishment before God. One can fix and describe the sign quite exactly but not the signified punishment and remission before God. The church cooperates in removing punishment only by helping the penitent to gain and to exercise a charity stirred by God's grace. The terms "satisfaction" and "treasury of the church" give only images of a personal process. Ultimately, God himself is the "treasury of the church," insofar as he accepts the church's intercession and our penitential efforts, to which he responds by reason of the merits of Christ.

All these statements on the theology of indulgences are to some extent based on recent historical research and theological reflection on the practice of ecclesiastical penance and indulgences by such men as Nikolaus Paulus,[5] Bernhard Poschmann,[6] and Karl Rahner.[7] In this historical study, theological reflection on the ultimate basis of indulgences has tended to follow and not to precede practice. This is not to say that developments in practice were not grounded theologically, although the grounds may not have been consciously grasped by the church. At any rate an adequate theology of indulgences must study them first in the historical context of penitential practice. This is the only way to understand them theologically and to set them in their proper place.

[5] Nikolaus Paulus, *Geschichte des Ablasses im Mittelalter*, 3 vols. (Paderborn: 1922–3).

[6] Bernhard Poschmann, *Der Ablass im Lichte der Bussgeschichte* (Bonn: 1948), and *Penance and the Annointing of the Sick*, translated and revised by Francis Courtney (London and New York: 1964), chaps. xv, xvi.

[7] "Remarks on the Theology of Indulgences," translated by Karl-H. Kruger in *Theological Investigations* (Baltimore and London: 1963), II, 175–98. This essay appeared first in a more compressed form in *Stimmen der Zeit*, CLVI (1955), 343–55. See also Rahner's article "Ablass" in *Lexikon für Theologie und Kirche* (2nd ed.), I, cols. 46–53.

From the beginning, ecclesiastical penance has been based on the belief that with the first signs of the will to do penance, the sinner is on the way to salvation, even though a long and difficult penitential process may lie before him. Guilt and punishment were in this early period not explicitly distinguished from one another. Since about the second century, the church as a community has given pastoral and intercessory support to the individual's personal efforts of penance. There developed eventually an ordered series of penitential practices corresponding to the gravity of the sin. These penances were assigned first in individual cases, but then became a part of a general system.

Another factor in penance was intercession of the martyrs, which was thought of as certain to be heard by God, but was only helpful to the extent that the penitent opened himself personally for God's cleansing and liberating grace. Where this intercession was made by a bishop as a representative of the church as a whole, the intercession was still not identical with the consequent reconciliation of the penitent with the church.

When practical and pastoral needs led to the custom of granting absolution immediately after confession of sins but before the work of penance, it was inevitable that the explicit distinction between guilt (*reatus culpae*) and punishment (*reatus poenae*) would become clearer in the church. There arose also an official intercession by the church which was independent of the penitential process itself. Further, change in cultural circumstances and consideration for the penitent himself led to more frequent use of commutations or redemptions by which one penitential work was substituted for another.

The early medieval intercessions or absolutions were solemn liturgical prayers or blessings in which the church interceded officially for penitents, often with explicit reference to a particular external work of penance. Thus, while redemptions touched the external, prescribed canonical penances, the intercessory absolutions were related to the punishment before

God. These two elements fused in the eleventh century to produce the first indulgences. But with an indulgence the penitential work did not have to be of the same gravity as was necessary in the case of the earlier commutations or redemptions. And the indulgence, in distinction to the intercessory absolutions, was an act of juridsiction. The juridical element touched the remission of canonical penalties, but at the same time the church's official prayer was directed to the remission of the corresponding punishment before God.

Bernhard Poschmann established the intercessory character of the early medieval absolutions. Since indulgences stem from these absolutions, Poschmann maintained that, in distinction to the jurisdictional and infallible effect of indulgences on ecclesiastical, canonical penalties, indulgences have only an intercessory, moral effectiveness in removing the punishments before God.[8] The objection arises quite naturally against Poschmann's position: In spite of the continuity between the early medieval absolutions and indulgences, could not the church have become aware subsequently of its jurisdictional powers to absolve from the punishments before God, i.e., of a power over and beyond mere intercession? Karl Rahner has answered this objection by pointing out that according to the Council of Trent (DS 1542, 1689, 1712) even the sacrament of penance does not free one from all temporal punishment, obviously because the church cannot absolve by an exercise of jurisdiction. But an indulgence cannot do more than the sacrament itself.[9] How could the church in the sacrament of penance do the greater act (forgive guilt) and not the lesser as well (free from punishment)? Rahner concludes that we must go beyond the conception of a purely vindictive punishment and stress the purgative nature of the punishments the sinner must undergo.[10] We must distinguish between the sinful deed and the consequent sinful attachment

[8] Poschmann, *Der Ablass im Lichte der Bussgeschichte*, pp. 43–62.

[9] Rahner, "Remarks on the Theology of Indulgences," *Theological Investigations*, II, 190ff.

[10] *Ibid.*, pp. 195–8.

caused by the sin. With forgiveness of the sin and remission of guilt, this inordinate *habitus* is not straightway removed. To destroy the *habitus*, penance and efforts toward a better life are necessary. Inordinacy stemming from sin is identical with concupiscence, which we can conceive furthermore as the penalty or punishment for the sin one is obliged to cleanse out in this life. This way of seeing the punishment for sin makes it conceivable that a soul would not want to be prematurely freed from punishment but would want further purification, as both St. Catherine of Genoa and Martin Luther maintained. On the other hand one can see how the prayer of the church for a penitent member could bring God to intensify and thereby shorten the process of purification.

What, though, was the situation in the Middle Ages as indulgences became common, especially regarding awareness of the need for penance and purification? It is clear that indulgences were seen as mitigating the earlier severity in penitential practice. Into the thirteenth century people viewed indulgences as a pastoral adaptation for the imperfect, and deeply earnest Christians would not in good conscience use them. The good work required in gaining an indulgence was not seen as penance but only as the more or less immediate extrinsic occasion for the church's intercession. The intercession thus began to function independently.

At this stage of indulgence practice theoretical reflection gradually set in. Early scholasticism did not derive the power of indulgences before God from the jurisdictional authority of the church. Just as with the earlier absolutions, indulgences were thought to work *per modum suffragii*. Moreover the role of the good work required in gaining an indulgence was not clear. It could be seen as only a condition, with the indulgence itself stemming from the church's jurisdiction over the penitential process. Or one could see indulgences in relation to the earlier redemptions and thus stress the substitution of one work for another. The canonist Huguccio (d. 1210) was the first to teach that an indulgence was formally a jurisdictional

The earliest likeness of Martin Luther, from an engraving of 1520
by Cranach the Elder in the Lutherhalle, Wittenberg

act of the church affecting the punishments before God. From the time of Hugo of St. Cher (ca. 1230) problems about the relative ease of the required work were answered by referring to the theological concept of the "treasury of the church." In this explanation, the power of indulgences before God stems from the merits of Christ and the good works the saints do under Christ's influence. Thirteenth-century scholasticism went one step further[11] in asserting that over and above the intercessory application of the merits of Christ and the saints, the church could also exercise jurisdiction in the strict sense by granting a particular person gaining an indulgence the benefits of the treasury. This often led to a predominantly commercial conception of the treasury of the church. Coupled with this was the fact that the indulgence system became more and more reserved to the pope, who claimed to have authority over this treasury of merit. In practice indulgences called attention only to vindictive punishments, and they appeared irrelevant to the work of inner purification. The need for personal receptiveness for remission of punishment was consequently underappreciated.

This tendency was further stimulated by the doctrine that indulgences could be applied to the dead; this doctrine can be traced to the thirteenth century, although papal grants of such indulgences came only in the mid-fifteenth century. Since the souls in purgatory are no longer under the church's jurisdiction, indulgences for them work *per modum suffragii*. St. Bonaventure could write, "Since they have left the forum of the church and of ecclesiastical judgment, it seems that no absolution can be granted them, except by way of intercession (*per modum deprecationis*). Thus, strictly speaking, they do not receive a remission of punishment."[12] Many

[11] See, for example, St. Thomas in the *Supplement to the Summa Theologiae*, questions 25–7. For Thomas an indulgence attains its effect *per modum dispensationis*.

[12] "Cum illi iam exierunt forum ecclesiae et ecclesiasticum iudicium, videtur, quod eis non possit fieri absolutio, nisi per modum deprecationis; et ita, proprie loquendo, non fit eis relaxatio." In *IV Sent.*, *d.* 20, *a.* 1, *q.* 5.

theologians, and especially the late medieval indulgence preachers, attributed nonetheless to the indulgence for the dead an absolutely certain effectiveness. In fact many based this idea precisely on the formula *per modum suffragii*, a phrase which for Bonaventure had had a clearly restrictive meaning.

In the last half of the fifteenth century, Gabriel Biel first saw the very possibility of an indulgence for the dead as an open question. To Biel's knowledge no statement had been made by the magisterium.[13] But he learned thereafter of Pope Sixtus IV's Bull of 1476 extending an indulgence for the Church of St. Peter in Saintes to the dead *per modum suffragii.*[14] Biel then explained in this way the phrase used by the pope, "It is not to be thought that this manner of intercession weakens the power of indulgences, as if, as some want it, the required work helped the souls no more than if it were offered for them and no indulgence were involved. The indulgence for the dead would in this case be given in vain; it would itself add nothing to the required work and the people would be deceived, an act which the church and the apostolic see would never allow."[15] For Biel, *per modum suffragii* excludes only the

[13] "Et nullibi apposite sunt conditiones per quas extenderetur ad purgandos in purgatorio. Estimo autem quod in casu huius dubii esset necessaria determinatio ecclesie." *Canonis Misse Expositio, lectio* 57 H, edited by Heiko A. Oberman and William J. Courtenay (Wiesbaden: 1965), II, 402.

[14] "Dum itaque illa scripsi, nondum venerat ad manus meas declaratio domini Sixti pape, novissime de medio sublati, qua declarat indulgentias proficere 'per modum suffragii' etiam animabus in purgatorio existentibus, dum ad ipsas per summum pontificem expresse extenduntur." *Ibid., lectio* 57 K, p. 402. The bull of Sixtus IV from 1476 and his explanation of the expression "*per modum suffragii*" in the following year are given in W. Köhler, *Dokumente zum Ablassstreit von 1517* (2nd ed.; Tübingen: 1934), pp. 37–40.

[15] "Et quod frequenter repetitum est 'per modum suffragii,' non est intelligendum quasi modus suffragii tollat efficaciam indulgentiarum, ita quod opus illud pro quo dantur indulgentie factum pro animabus, non plus valeat animabus quam si idem opus vel suffragium factum esset pro eis, nullis indulgentiis adiunctis, sicut quidam intelligere voluerunt. Sic enim frustra daretur indulgentia pro animabus, nihil enim proficeret nec aliquid suffragio impenso superadderet, et per huiusmodi indulgentiarum concessionem populus deciperetur, quod de ecclesia et de sede apostolica est nullatenus presumendum." Biel, *Canonis Misse Expositio, lectio* 57 L, Oberman-Courtenay ed., II, 403.

judicial power the church has over the living. Since the departed cannot perform an external work of penance, this must be supplied by the living. "The work of another comes to their aid (*suffragatur eis*), so that they can gain an indulgence. The indulgence then is of no less value than if they had personally performed the work."[16] Biel can therefore paraphrase "*per modum suffragii*" as "on the basis of a work done by another and then applied to them."[17] For instance, if a poor man cannot take part in a crusade to which an indulgence is attached, but if a friend sends a mercenary in his name, then the poor man gains the indulgence *per modum suffragii*.[18] This conception of *suffragium* as *subsidium* was shared by the papal commissioner for indulgences, Raimund Peraudi (d. 1505). Since the souls in purgatory could not make a financial contribution, living persons must make it for them.[19]

From this point it was only a short step to the doctrine taught in Peraudi's treatise of 1488 "*Modus promerendi indulgentias*" that confession and a visit to a church were not required for gaining an indulgence for the dead, but that the contribution of alms alone sufficed.[20] The Sorbonne had unanimously rejected this interpretation in 1482,[21] but the

[16] "Cum autem huiusmodi opus defuncti adimplere non possunt, dum illud fit pro eis ab alio, iam opus alterius suffragatur eis, ut possint consequi indulgentias, non minus si ipsi per se opus illud implevissent." *Ibid.*, p. 404.

[17] ". . . per modum suffragii, id est propter aliquod opus ab alio factum, et eis per modum suffragii applicatum." *Ibid.*

[18] "Et alius suus amicus pro paupere sive pauperis nomine mitteret, iam pauperi proficerent indulgentie per modum suffragii." *Ibid.*

[19] Paulus, *Geschichte des Ablasses im Mittelalter*, III, 385.

[20] T. Freudenberger, *Der Würzburger Domprediger Dr. Johann Reyss* (Münster: 1954), p. 91.

[21] Paulus, *Geschichte des Ablasses im Mittelalter*, III, 386. Also the *Summa de casibus conscientiae* by Angelus Carletus de Clavasio (d. about 1495) demands the state of grace as a condition for gaining an indulgence for the departed: "Requiritur tamen si debet valere pro alio quod tam ille qui accipit quam ille pro quo acciputur sint in statu gratie. Aliter valeret neque per modum indulgentiae neque per modum suffragii." From chapter 22 of Carletus' entry "*Indulgentia.*" This book was popularly known as the "*Summa angelica*" and was burned by Luther on December 10, 1520, along with the papal bull threatening him with excommunication. The Weimar edition of Luther's works has in one place (W 42, 486, 32) mistakenly identified the "*Summa angelica*" as the *Summa* of St. Thomas.

rejection could hardly overcome the implications of the conception of *suffragium* held by Biel, Peraudi, and others. Johannes Eck saw the *per modum suffragii* not as diminishing but as increasing the effectiveness of indulgences,[22] an idea that was popular at the beginning of the sixteenth century, though it was not unopposed.

Added to this theology of indulgences, there was on the eve of the Reformation a decided externalizing of the good work required in gaining an indulgence. Both Biel and Altenstaig (in a popular theological dictionary published in December 1517) followed Duns Scotus in stressing excessively the physical difficulty of a work of satisfaction.[23] Even one in mortal sin can perform such a work of satisfaction for punishment, although he cannot thereby merit grace and glory. Where Scotus expressly excluded the possibility that a person in mortal sin could by an external work attain reconciliation with God, here Altenstaig is not so clear.

The liturgical pomp of the solemn acts of penance connected with indulgences could not hide the increasing loss of religious substance. This liturgy seems rather to have served only to attract popular attention.

A special factor in the development of indulgences was the growing financial importance they had in the late Middle Ages,[24] which stemmed from the introduction of almsgiving as the good work required for gaining an indulgence. In itself this was not objectionable, but there was danger that financial considerations could become dominant in the indulgence system, partly because of the contemporary shift from a barter economy to a money economy. The alms came to be viewed as a source of funds for the official granting the indul-

[22] Johannes Eck wrote in his critical remarks, the "*Obelisci*," on Luther's indulgence theses, "*illa (particula per modum suffragii) non diminuat (ut vult positor), sed potius addat* . . ." Given in W 1, 296.

[23] Scotus, in *IV Sent.*, *d.* 15, *q.* 1; Biel, in *IV Sent.*, *d.* 16, *q.* 2, *a.* 1, *not.* 1 C; Altenstaig, s.v. "*Satisfactio*" in *Vocabularius Theologiae* (Hagenau: 1517).

[24] On the following, see Paulus, *Geschichte des Ablasses im Mittelalter*, III, 450–69, and J. Hashagen, *Staat und Kirche vor der Reformation* (Essen: 1931), pp. 162–79.

gence. Thus churchmen could treat indulgences in terms of financial need or simply of prestige. The jubilee indulgences proved to be especially profitable for the Roman curia. The granting of indulgences was held within reasonable limits for a time, but the Great Schism led to an uncontrolled multiplication of indulgences, with Rome and Avignon striving to outdo each other in the indulgences they offered.

Territorial considerations grew more important in the indulgence system as cities and princedoms gave their allegiance to pope or antipope. This prepared the way for the "indulgence authority" of local princes, who became concerned over the serious financial problem posed by the flow of money given as alms for indulgences out of their territories.

Indulgences became a kind of special tax for projects of common benefit. The proceeds from indulgences were used to support military campaigns (which were by no means always against pagans or heretics), or for building dikes and bridges. Princes thought of themselves as administrators of indulgences granted by the church, and so strove to share in the income. The support of the local prince for an indulgence could be a decisive factor for its success, and those indulgences which did not fit into the financial plans of the prince or which were feared as too strong competitors for some local shrine could be excluded from a territory. Mistrust of the curia, combined with the role of civil authority in administering and profiting from indulgences, led to complicated and amazing arrangements in applying the money gained through indulgences. For instance, in the jubilee bull "*Domini et salvatoris,*" Pope Alexander VI granted an indulgence in support of a campaign against the Turks, for which the Cardinal of Gurk, Raimund Peraudi, was commissioned as chief administrator. The cardinal-legate then had to negotiate with both the emperor and with the council of regency before the indulgence could be introduced into Germany. Emperor Maximilian gave his approval in April 1501, but ordered that the money be deposited in the banks of the Fugger and Welser

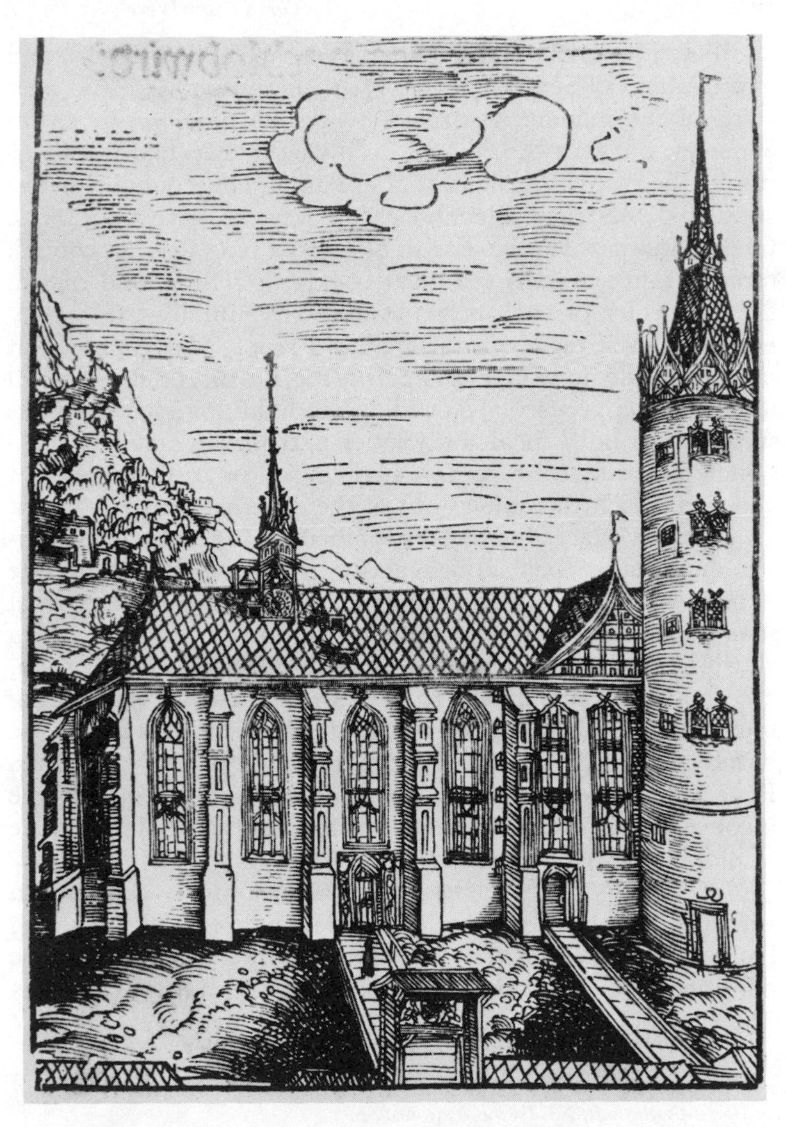

The castle church in Wittenberg, from an engraving of 1509
by Cranach the Elder in the Lutherhalle, Wittenberg

families. The council of regency agreed to the indulgence and in a contract of September 11, 1501, they stipulated that one-third of the income was to go to the cardinal to cover his expenses, but that the council itself would keep two-thirds for use in the campaign against the Turks. The council further stipulated that the collection chests were to have four locks. One key went to the cardinal-legate, one to the council representative, one to the local bishop or pastor, and one to the civil ruler of each community.[25] Eventually the money not drained off at the local level did reach Maximilian, but since he made no campaign against the Turks, it did not fulfill its original purpose.[26] Nor did Cardinal Peraudi gain his share, since both local authorities and his own subcommissioners refused, so he complained, to follow instructions but chose to enrich themselves out of the contributions.[27]

In many places local rulers gained an indulgence monopoly and made their approval for a particular indulgence dependent on their own share in the income. Their usual share was one-third of the contributions from any given church, but they frequently took, with or without permission, the one-third earmarked for the pope.[28] In 1508 King Sigismund of Poland wanted to refuse to admit into his realm the indulgence for the new St. Peter's. He relented however when Pope Julius II agreed that he could keep two-thirds of the income for his own defense program against the Turks. The same arrangement was made in Hungary.[29]

In early 1517 Duke George of Saxony finally reached an agreement with his cousin Prince-elector Frederick and with Duke John the Elder that no Roman indulgences were to be admitted into their territories except after mutual consulta-

[25] A.Schulte, *Die Fugger in Rom (1495–1523)* (Leipzig: 1904), I, 42.

[26] *Ibid.*, p. 259ff.

[27] Paulus, "Raimund Peraudi als Ablasskommisar," *Historisches Jahrbuch der Görres-Gesellschaft*, XXI (1900), p. 681, n. 1.

[28] Hashagen, *Staat und Kirche vor der Reformation*, p. 171.

[29] Schulte, *Die Fugger in Rom*, I, 47; Paulus, *Geschichte des Ablasses im Mittelalter*, III, 171f.; Hashagen, *Staat und Kirche vor der Reformation*, p. 174.

tion.[30] Duke George was especially eager to exclude all other indulgences from his territory because Pope Leo X had granted an indulgence to the Saxon city of Annaberg which Julius II had refused to do. However, it would have been of little use for Duke George to suppress other indulgences in his own territory if his subjects could gain them across the border in the areas ruled by Prince Frederick or Duke John.[31]

Today state lotteries are often held for the care of ancient churches and monuments or for charitable purposes, with the state taking part of the income. Similarly, at the end of the Middle Ages indulgences intended to support ecclesiastical institutions were no less favored by princes in need of money.

Thus we find a growing secularization of indulgences which quite naturally gave rise to popular suspicion of financial exploitation under a pretext of religion. The excessive multiplication of indulgences led to efforts to reduce their number—efforts which were not always based on purely religious motives.

Financial exploitation of indulgences by both ecclesiastical and civil authorities further suppressed the awareness that an indulgence contribution was an alms for a charitable or liturgical purpose. Thus it became all the easier to set indulgence contributions and alms against each other and to argue, as Luther did, that alms and works of charity are incomparably more valuable than indulgences.[32]

[30] *Akten und Briefe zur Kirchenpolitik Herzog Georgs von Sachsen*, edited by F. Gess (Leipzig: 1905), I, 3ff.

[31] The Franciscan Thomas Murner satirized the "indulgence authority" of the princes in his "Conspiracy of Fools" in 1512: "Wil der papst ein ablass geben,/So nimmt der herr sein teil so neben;/Wolt man im sein teil nit lohnen, /So muss der ablass bleiben stohnen." Thomas Murner, *Deutsche Schriften*, edited by M. Spanier (Berlin: 1926), II, 249 (slightly modernized).

[32] From Luther's letter to Spalatin (February 2, 1518), WBr 1, 146, 63. See also Luther's indulgence theses 41–5.

II. ORIGIN OF THE CONTROVERSY OF 1517

On April 4, 1506, Pope Julius II laid the cornerstone of the new St. Peter's basilica. To finance this mammoth project he granted a plenary indulgence in 1507, which his successor Leo X renewed upon becoming pope in 1513. A grant was no guarantee that an indulgence would actually be preached because of the frequent opposition of local church and civil authorities. The St. Peter's indulgence granted by Julius II was at first not allowed in Germany, lest it conflict with an indulgence granted the Teutonic order in Livonia to support its defense against Russian attacks. A similar crusade indulgence in Portugal excluded the St. Peter's indulgence, and an indulgence for the church in Saintes excluded it in France.[1]

Special circumstances under Leo X, however, led to the introduction of the St. Peter's indulgence in roughly half of Germany, i.e., in the ecclesiastical provinces of Mainz and Magdeburg, in the civil territories of the bishop of these two cities, of the bishop of Halberstadt, and of the margrave of Brandenburg. Albrecht, the twenty-three-year-old younger brother of Prince-elector Joachim I of Brandenburg, had become archbishop of Magdeburg and administrator of the diocese of Halberstadt in 1513. Less than a year later, the cathedral chapter of Mainz nominated this easygoing Hohenzollern prince as archbishop and prince-elector of Mainz. Albrecht was the third prince-bishop to be named in Mainz within a decade, and the diocese was not able to pay once again the nomination taxes and the pallium fee; Albrecht

[1] Paulus, *Geschichte des Ablasses im Mittelalter*, III, 172f.

therefore agreed to pay the needed 14,000 ducats himself. Since young Albrecht wanted to continue ruling the dioceses of Magdeburg and Halberstadt, there was the further question of 10,000 ducats for a dispensation from the law against the cumulation of benefices.[2] As the humanist Konrad Mutian wrote cynically to a friend, "Is there anything that one cannot purchase in Rome?"[3] The curia agreed to grant Albrecht's request for this dispensation, which was an extraordinary one both for the times and for so young a man. The dispensation fee of 10,000 ducats was applied to the building of St. Peter's. Albrecht did not have funds on hand to pay the 24,000 ducats, and he was already in debt to the Fuggers of Augsburg for the papal confirmation of his nomination in Magdeburg. But he was able to contract a further loan from them of 29,000 gold florins.[4] The curia indicated the way Albrecht could pay his debts. If he were to allow the St. Peter's indulgence to be preached in his territories for eight years, he could keep half of the income. If we include the 2,143 ducats the emperor demanded from Albrecht, his total debt was 26,143 ducats. Therefore, if the indulgence were to be successful, it had to bring in a grand total of 52,286 ducats.[5]

Pope Leo X's bull "*Sacrosanctis Salvatoris et Redemptoris nostri*"[6] granted permission for preaching the plenary indulgence for eight years in order to bring about the "necessary reconstruction of the basilica of the Prince of the Apostles." The only real reason this indulgence came to be preached in

[2] Schulte, *Die Fugger in Rom*, I, 97–141; G. von Pölnitz, *Jakob Fugger* (Tübingen: 1949), I, 307–11 and II, 324–7.

[3] "Unus iuvenis vix paedagogos et rudimenta literarum reliquens uno anno fit ter praesul, et quidem eminentissimus. Miror, si Leo X daenam (vulgo pallium vocant) transmittat. Sed Romae quid non venale?" From *Der Briefwechsel des Conrad Mutianus*, edited by K. Gillert (Halle: 1880), I, 104. See also Hans Volz, "Erzbischof Albrecht von Mainz und Martin Luthers 95 Thesen," *Jahrbuch der Hessischen kirchengeschichtlichen Vereinigung*, XIII (1962), p. 191, n. 10.

[4] Schulte, *Die Fugger in Rom*, I, 104. According to von Pölnitz the Fuggers lent Albrecht a grand total of 50,000 gold florins to cover his debts in Rome. *Jakob Fugger*, I, 310.

[5] Schulte, *Die Fugger in Rom*, I, 140.

[6] Köhler, *Dokumente*, pp. 83–93.

Germany was the desire of Albrecht to pay the debts he accrued in buying himself a series of episcopal sees. The indulgence became thereby a "bartering piece in a business transaction."[7] Whether this was formally simony or not is a purely speculative question. "The whole affair was," as we must with shame agree, "a notorious scandal."[8]

As commissioner for the indulgence, Albrecht published the usual extensive instructions for his subcommissioners, for the preachers, and for confessors.[9] The document is not an original composition but follows earlier instructions and in its main lines is identical with the instructions on the St. Peter's indulgence written by Giovannangelo Arcimboldi in 1515.[10]

Albrecht's "*Instructio summaria*" gives directions on the conduct and life of the indulgence preachers, on the times and places of their sermons, on the money to be paid (with details adapting this requirement to various economic levels of society), on the age and social class of penitents, on the many graces of the indulgence, and on the powers granted to commute vows and duties of restitution. Just as in Arcimboldi's instructions, four principal graces are listed, each of which can be gained without the others.

> The first grace is the complete remission of all sins. No greater grace than this can be conceived, for here the sinner who was deprived of God's grace receives again the grace of God, through a perfect remission. This remission of sins frees one completely from the punishments due in purgatory for offending the divine majesty, and in fact wholly wipes out these punishments.[11]

Later the *instructio* speaks of contrition and confession, or at least the intention thereto, as the first condition for gaining

[7] J. Lortz, *Die Reformation in Deutschland* (4th ed.; Freiburg: 1962), I, 199.

[8] K. A. Meissinger, *Der katholische Luther* (Munich: 1952), p. 129.

[9] The text of this, the "*Instructio summaria*," is given in Köhler, *Dokumente*, pp. 104–24.

[10] A German translation of Arcimboldi's instruction is given in the Walch edition of Luther's works (St. Louis: 1899), XV, 256–77. On Arcimboldi, see *Lexikon für Theologie und Kirche* (2nd ed.), vol. I, col. 827f.

[11] Köhler, *Dokumente*, p. 110, ll. 24–30.

the indulgence. Still, it is not sufficiently clear that the indulgence itself does not remit sins, but only that the punishment for sins for which one is contrite and which have been absolved is remitted.

The second principal grace of the indulgence also draws attention to the forgiveness of sins. For this grace is a confessional letter, valid even after the eight-year period of the indulgence, with which a person can confess to any priest he might choose and be absolved by him from sins reserved to the pope.

> The second principal grace is a confessional letter granting faculties more magnanimously than ever before, retaining its validity even after the expiration of the eight-year period stipulated for this bull. . . . Those who purchase this letter are granted the freedom to choose a suitable confessor, even [one] from a mendicant order, who then can absolve them from all censures . . . and from the most serious sins, even from those reserved to the holy see, and this once during their lives and at the hour of death.[12]

> The third principal grace is a participation in all goods of the universal church. This means that those who contribute to this building project, as well as their deceased parents who died in the love of God, will now and in perpetuity share in all petitions, intercessions, alms, fasts, prayers, pilgrimages of all kinds, even to the Holy Land, and in [the visits to] the stational churches in Rome, in masses, canonical hours, disciplines, and all other spiritual good works that are done and can be done in the universal, most holy, church militant and by all her members. The faithful obtain this participation when they purchase a confessional letter.[13]

It was explicitly stressed that to gain this third grace one did not need to go to confession or to visit the designated churches and altars, but only to purchase the confessional

[12] *Ibid.*, p. 113, l. 19 to p. 114, l. 6. There is here no offer of forgiveness of future sins, as Luther later stated—or at least as he was misunderstood to have said (See WTr 5, 657f., n. 6431). Rather, the permission was given to approach the confessor of one's choice, even for confessing sins reserved to the pope.

[13] Köhler, *Dokumente*, p. 115, ll. 20–30.

letter.[14] This stipulation is all the more questionable since it gave the impression that it was on the basis of the confessional letter that one gained his share in the spiritual goods of the church. Thus, one in mortal sin who purchased a confessional letter would appear to gain something that could come only to a living member of the body of Christ. Luther attacked this idea in his indulgence theses 35 and 37.[15]

> The fourth principal grace is the complete remission of all sins granted to the souls in purgatory. The pope grants and confers this remission to the souls in purgatory by way of intercession (*per modum suffragii*), in such wise that the contribution made on their behalf by the living has the effect it would have if they had done it themselves. . . . It is not necessary that those making the contribution be contrite and have confessed, since this fourth grace is based on a combination of the charity in which the departed person died and the contribution made by a living person, as is clear in the bull granting the indulgence.[16] The preachers should be most diligent in effectively describing this grace, since it will most certainly aid the departed souls and will be most fruitful in gaining support for the building of St. Peter's.[17]

The last sentence promotes the use of the opinion which

[14] "Declaramus etiam, quod pro dictis duabus gratiis principalibus consequendis non est opus confiteri seu ecclesias aut altaria visitare, sed dumtaxat confessionale redimere." *Ibid.*, p. 116, ll. 1–3.

[15] Thesis 35: "They who teach that contrition is not necessary on the part of those who intend to buy souls out of purgatory or to buy confessional privileges preach unchristian doctrine." Thesis 37: "Any true Christian, whether living or dead, participates in all the blessings of Christ and the church; and this is granted him by God even without indulgence letters." LW 31, 28f. (C. M. Jacobs and Harold J. Grimm).

[16] In the bull granting the indulgence Leo X had explained that the departed who needed prayers and were unable to help themselves could receive help out of the treasury of the church and that a plenary indulgence would be granted them by way of intercession when someone out of piety gave the stipulated alms on their behalf. It was not said that the donor did not need to be in the state of grace for this: "*. . . eadem plenissima indulgentia per modum suffragii animabus ipsis in purgatorio existentibus, pro quibus dictam eleemosynam pie erogari contigerit, ut praefertur, pro plenaria poenarum relaxatione suffragetur.*" Köhler, *Dokumente*, p. 92, ll. 23–6. See also Luther's Thesis 35.

[17] *Ibid.*, p. 116, ll. 16–32.

was charged as suspect at the Sorbonne in 1482,[18] and which had a popular form in the couplet, "When the coin in the basket clings, then the soul from the fire springs." The faithful were in effect led to postpone penance, and the impression was strengthened that the real concern of indulgences was money and not the salvation of souls.

It may have been that the doctrine contained in the "*Instructio summaria*" was technically within the somewhat sketchy limits of official church teaching on indulgences. In practice the *instructio* lent support to various abuses and misunderstandings, and its frequent use of pious superlatives led to a highly commercialized extolling of indulgences. The *instructio* was unabashedly directed toward the highest possible financial return from the St. Peter's indulgences.

The preachers were to make it clear to their hearers "how necessary the indulgence graces were for a man desirous of eternal life."[19] The preachers were to point out "the boundless and inestimable benefits of indulgences"[20] and to warn people against neglecting or despising the unprecedented apostolic powers of the present indulgence because of earlier indulgences and their benefits.[21] The *instructio* mentioned more than once the unprecedented powers of the indulgence to grant an extraordinary release from punishment.[22] It is noteworthy that the parallel texts in Arcimboldi's instruction did not use the deceptive exaggerations (such as "unprecedented") and the superlatives of Albrecht's text. The faithful who already possessed confessional letters from earlier indulgences were to be urged nonetheless to purchase a new letter, because of the new graces granted now, which previous letters had not given.[23] "Previously the apostolic see has never

[18] Paulus, *Geschichte des Ablasses im Mittelalter*, III, 386. Also, Paulus, *Johann Tetzel der Ablassprediger* (Mainz: 1899), pp. 162f. See above, p. 12, n. 21.

[19] Köhler, *Dokumente*, p. 107, l. 33.

[20] *Ibid.*, p. 108, l. 1.

[21] *Ibid.*, p. 109, l. 17.

[22] *Ibid.*, p. 113, l. 22.

[23] *Ibid.*, p. 116, l. 7.

granted such generous dispensations, commutations, and compensations."[24]

In setting the amounts people were to contribute in order to gain the indulgence, the confessors were always to keep in mind the aim of greater support for St. Peter's and to urge their penitents to contribute even more. However, no one was to be sent away without some benefit from the graces of the indulgence, since the whole project was to aid the salvation of the Christian faithful no less than to support the building of St. Peter's. Therefore prayers and fasting could be substituted for a financial contribution. For the kingdom of heaven must be no less open to the poor than to the rich.[25] There are in the *instructio* remarks that would exclude the worst abuses, but a pressing concern for the highest possible financial return is the dominant theme, a point all the more repulsive to one who knows that Albrecht personally received half of the money contributed.

A final stipulation was that other sermons were not to be held in a town while the indulgence was being preached.[26] The aim here was surely not that the faithful attend all the more to their salvation through the great graces of the indulgence, but simply that there be no competition to hurt the lucrative selling of indulgences. Luther attacked this stipulation sharply in his letter to Albrecht on October 31, 1517, and in his thesis 53. Throughout, the "*Instructio summaria*" reflects a pernicious fusion of financial motivation with spiritual largess. This fusion was in itself quite questionable and led to the further danger that in practice the baser motivation would become dominant and tend to suppress the spiritual aims.

On January 22, 1517, the Leipzig Dominican, Johannes Tetzel, was appointed one of two subcommissioners for

[24] *Ibid.*, p. 117, l. 1ff. In the parallel in Arcimboldi's instruction this exaggerated formulation is missing. See the Walch edition of Luther's works, XV, 318.

[25] Köhler, *Dokumente*, p. 112, l. 27 to p. 113, l. 2.

[26] *Ibid.*, p. 107, l. 25.

preaching the indulgence for St. Peter's in the ecclesiastical province of Magdeburg, a work for which he was to be well compensated.[27] Tetzel had already preached an indulgence in support of the Teutonic order of knights in 1504–10 in the Naumburg and Merseburg dioceses, on the lower Rhein, in Saxony, Silesia, Alsace, and in Franconia. Before taking the post under Albrecht, Tetzel had preached the St. Peter's indulgence in the diocese of Meissen in 1516 under the nuncio Arcimboldi.

After his appointment by Albrecht, Tetzel, in early February 1517, began preaching the St. Peter's indulgence in the Dominican church in Leipzig. He is reported to have given out no confessional letters in Leipzig and to have taken no money because of the stubborn opposition of the local ruler, Duke George of Saxony.[28] Tetzel then moved westward into towns in the civil territory of the bishop of Merseburg. In March he preached in Halle in the archdiocese of Magdeburg, and on April 10 he was in Jüterbog, only eighteen miles from Wittenberg.[29] In 1540 Luther himself narrated, "At this time Tetzel brought the indulgence as far as Jüterbog, but our prince [Frederick the Wise] would not admit him. But a huge crowd of people heard him, and what they heard went around in Wittenberg, e.g., 'If a man had violated the Virgin Mary, my indulgence would still be great enough to help him,' and 'I have more power for forgiving than Saints Peter and Paul together.' "[30] Luther reported that the peo-

[27] Volz, *Martin Luthers Thesenanschlag und dessen Vorgeschichte* (Weimar: 1959), p. 11, nn. 11, 12. According to A. Schulte, Tetzel and his agents were paid more than three hundred florins a month. *Die Fugger in Rom*, I, 150. On December 13, 1517, Albrecht complained in a letter to his Magdeburg councillors about the high demands of the subcommissioners. Paulus, *Johann Tetzel*, p. 119.

[28] Gess, ed., *Akten und Briefe zur Kirchenpolitik Herzog Georgs von Sachsen*, I, 1–5.

[29] Paulus, *Johann Tetzel*, p. 41; Volz, *Martin Luthers Thesenanschlag und dessen Vorgeschichte*, p. 13.

[30] WTr 5, 77, n. 5349. Luther narrated this version of Tetzel's preaching in his letter to Archibishop Albrecht on October 31, 1517. (WBr 1, 110, 21ff.) Tetzel quite emphatically denied having said this about Our Lady in the seventy-fourth of the theses against Luther which he defended in Frankfurt on the Oder in January, 1518. Paulus, *Johann Tetzel*, pp. 57, 177.

ple of Wittenbergran "like madmen" over to Tetzel in Jüterbog.[31]

Luther's sovereign, Frederick the Wise, had refused to admit the St. Peter's indulgence into Wittenberg and the rest of his Saxon domain. Earlier, the dioceses of Magdeburg and Halberstadt had been ruled by younger princes of Frederick's own family, but now the rival Hohenzollern family had taken them over and had acquired the lands of the grand master of the Teutonic order as well. Albrecht's election as archbishop of Magdeburg had thus swung the balance of power in northern and central Germany from the Saxon house to that of the Hohenzollerns.[32] Frederick was therefore adamant that the money of his Saxon subjects should not, through the St. Peter's indulgence, accrue to the rival of his own house. In addition, this indulgence would have offered competition too strong for Frederick's own beloved pilgrimage Church of All Saints in Wittenberg with its rich collection of relics and generous endowment of indulgences for pilgrims.[33]

Tetzel's private life gave no cause for complaint. He was not one of the indulgence preachers whom both Luther and Johannes Eck charged with paying their prostitutes with indulgence certificates.[34] But still Tetzel was one in whom the drive for financial gain dominated over preaching contrition and sorrow, as Johannes Cochläus, Hieronymus Emser, and Duke George of Saxony all complained.[35] Emser, the court chaplain for Duke George, wrote in 1521, "No one should question that this indulgence itself is good, justified, and to be respected. . . . The abuses are no fault of the pope but stem

[31] WTr 5, 76, n. 5346; W 51, 539; W 30II, 282ff.; WTr 5, 535, n. 6201.

[32] Volz, "Erzbischof Albrecht von Mainz und Martin Luthers 95 Thesen," *Jahrbuch der Hessischen kirchengeschichtlichen Vereinigung*, XIII (1962), p. 192f.

[33] P. Kirn, *Friedrich der Weise und die Kirche* (Leipzig and Berlin: 1926), p. 130f. See also *Wittemberger Heiligthumsbuch* (Wittenberg: 1509), in *Liebhaberbibliothek alter Illustratoren in Facsimile-Reproduction* VI (Munich: 1884).

[34] W 1, 588, 29f. Eck, in his reform schema for the pope, in *Acta reformationis catholicae*, edited by G. Pfeilschifter (Regensburg: 1959), I, 110.

[35] Paulus, *Johann Tetzel*, p. 117f., and *Geschichte des Ablasses im Mittelalter*, III, 483.

from the avarice of the friars and priests serving as commissioners. Their shameless preaching aims only at getting money and filling their coffers to the brim. They exaggerate and stress money more than confession, contrition, and sorrow. For this they have surely no commission from his holiness the pope."[36]

Another contemporary witness, Johann Linder, a Dominican of Pirna, reports this about Tetzel: "He thought of unheard of ways to take in money, reduced the conditions for gaining the indulgence, and erected very ordinary crosses in the towns and villages. Eventually, this offended the common folk themselves and they came to despise this great spiritual treasure and to complain about these abuses."[37]

Luther encountered the results of Tetzel's preaching as he heard the ideas and expectations that had been planted in the minds of his own penitents. People from Wittenberg who had heard Tetzel's sermons in Jüterbog had bought confessional letters and then brought them to Luther in the confessional. Friedrich Myconius in his chronicle of 1541–42 tells that Luther became aware of the disastrous effects of the indulgence sermons when penitents demanded absolution—independently of any sign of contrition and purpose of amendment—just because they had a confessional letter.[38]

This stimulated Luther, as he himself said, "gradually to warn people against the indulgence and to explain to them what grace and the forgiveness of sins really were."[39]

[36] Hieronymus Emser, *Wider das unchristliche buch Martini Luthers Augustiners an den Tewtschen Adel aussgangen* (Leipzig: 1521), cited from Paulus, *Johann Tetzel*, p. 117.

[37] Cited by Paulus, *Ibid.*, p. 120.

[38] Friedrich Myconius, *Geschichte der Reformation*, edited by O. Clemen (Leipzig: n. d.), p. 20f.

[39] WTr 5, 76, n. 4346.

III. LUTHER ON INDULGENCES

LUTHER HAD ALREADY DEALT critically with indulgences in the years before 1517. In his first lectures on the Psalms in 1513–15 he pointed to the danger of a false security about one's salvation to which the doctrine and practice of indulgences could give rise among the faithful. "By indulgences we make the way to heaven extremely easy." (W 3, 416, 21f.) This false security is the root evil of the times (W 3, 430, 36ff.), an evil that leads to tepidity and further sins. (W 3, 416, 17f., 29f. and 417, 10–22)

Luther saw Satan attacking the church through this false sense of security and through spiritual drowsiness in an attack more devastating than any of his attacks in the times of the persecutions. Christians, he wrote, are like heirs who wastefully spend their heritage without adding to it. Popes and bishops shower the faithful with graces and indulgences without care for their spiritual benefit from these gifts. The *thesaurus* of the church may be unlimited, but a person can only share in this by making some contribution himself.[1] In other words, an indulgence, as a support for our penance, could benefit only a truly penitent man. The norm governing the number of indulgences and indulgenced confraternities in Luther's day was not the good of souls but the daily needs and even the avarice of prelates and mendicant friars. Luther saw

[1] "Accipere enim de thesauro Ecclesiae et non addere est impossibile et frustranea praesumptio. . . . Non quod thesaurus Ecclesiae sit consumptibilis, sed nobis dico consumptibilis. Est enim infinitus in se, sed non in nobis, quia minor pars eo participat." W 3, 424, 22ff.

the desolating sacrilege set up in the holy place, as foretold in Matt. 24:15. (W 3, 425, 7ff.)

Luther's criticism was sharp, but it was not directed against indulgences in themselves nor against the doctrine of the treasury of the church, but rather against irresponsible pastoral practice.

While lecturing on Romans in 1515–16, Luther apparently referred to Pope Leo's bull of March 31, 1515, extending the St. Peter's indulgence to the territories under Archbishop Albrecht's rule. Luther stressed that faith in God's word is decisive for a good work rather than the external work itself. The observation led to criticism of the preachers who made much of impressive external works and their imitation. "This gives rise to the many promises and grants of indulgences for building and decorating churches and for multiplying ceremonies. In all this they make no least mention of how each man should be serving God in his own state in life." (W 56, 417, 23ff.) On the one hand the pope and bishops are extremely generous with indulgences in return for contributions for the building of churches, but on the other hand they are quite miserly in giving freely for the help of souls what they have freely received. (W 56, 417, 27ff.)

Luther appears to have made an indirect reference to the twenty-five-year-old Albrecht when he charged youthful princes and effeminate rulers in the church with using tyrannical force and harshness on their subjects instead of seeking to make them first of all ready and willing to serve. (W 56, 502, 10ff.)

Among Luther's extant early sermons, two treat of indulgences.[2] In the sermon for St. Matthias' Day, February 24, 1517, he stressed that since Christ alone is our righteousness,

[2] A third reference to indulgences occurs in the sermon for the feast of the Purification of Our Lady, dated February 2, 1517, by the Weimar edition. Two versions of this sermon are extant: W 1, 130ff. and W 4, 636ff. Luther treats Rom. 1:17 in this sermon, and has this to say about indulgences: "omnis scriptura sonare videtur unicum verbum de indulgentiis, quod est credere in Christum. Haec sunt verissimae indulgentiae." W 4, 636, 28.

our own efforts will not bring peace of conscience. The one way to peace is to understand "that the grace and mercy of God are given us out of pure grace in Christ as his merits are imputed to us." (W 1, 140, 29f.) But to gain this peace we must become detached from ourselves, something none fears more than he who is set on achieving purity from sin by his own efforts. Luther found such false zeal actually directed more against the punishments for sin than against sin itself. As long as sin itself remains, the anguish of conscience remains. But one detached from self and filled with hatred for sin need not fear, since the removal of guilt wiped out the punishment as well, he said.

Indulgences tended to support self seeking, which for Luther was the essence of sin, and the "servile justice" stemming from self seeking. "Indulgences teach people to fear, flee, and avoid the punishment for sin, but not the sin itself." (W 1, 141, 23f.) Instead, people should be taught to love punishment and to embrace the cross. Indulgences should at best be granted only to the weak in faith, so as not to disturb those living under the cross and thereby attaining to meekness, humility, and eventually to peace of soul. (Matt. 11:29) Luther concluded, "True meekness is found only in penance and at the cross," but indulgences free man from penance, and train us to avoid the cross. Thus they impede our efforts to become meek and humble of heart, that is, to attain true indulgence by coming to Christ. Luther ended his sermon with this outburst: "Oh, the dangers besetting us today! Oh, you snoring priests! Oh, the darkness worse than Egypt! We are surrounded by ruinous evils, and how we loll in false security!" (W 1, 141, 34ff.)

Another early sermon is entitled "*Sermo de indulgentiis pridie dedicationis*" and has been variously dated October 31, 1516, and October 31, 1517. Two versions of this sermon have been handed down: one in V. E. Löscher's 1720 edition of Reformation records and documents[3] where the sermon was

[3] *Vollständige Reformationis acta und Documenta* (Leipzig: 1720), I, 734–40.

On Aplas von Rom
kan man wol selig werden 
durch anzaigung der götlichen
hailigen geschrifft.

Pamphlet title page written at the beginning of the Reformation with an illustration showing the sale of indulgences taken from a manuscript since lost (W 1, 94–9), and a second version in a copy made by an auditor of the sermon which was found in the library in Zwickau. (W 4, 670–4) Only the title of the sermon gives us evidence regarding the date: "*Sermo de indulgentiis pridie dedicationis*" (W 1, 94, 5f.) or "*In die dedicationis templi sermo.*" (W 4, 670, 1) Scholars agree that the sermon was given on October 31 or on November 1. Löscher gave 1517 as the year, but J. K. F. Knaake, the editor of the first volume of the Weimar edition, gave 1516. All others, with the exception of Karl Bauer,[4] have followed the earlier dating. Knaake's argument was that even according to Löscher the sermon was part of Luther's series of sermons on the Ten Commandments, a series that closed on February 2, 1517. Therefore, it would have been given in November, 1516. However, there are good reasons for a later date: first, because of the more developed stage of Luther's criticism of indulgences; second, because the sermon is directed against the indulgence preaching of Tetzel and not against the indulgences for pilgrims to the castle church in Wittenberg; and third, because of the similarities between Luther's sermon and the ninety-five theses. These facts point to mid 1517 or late 1517 as the date of the sermon. Furthermore, there is no convincing reason for the sermon having been given in the castle church. Luther's early sermons on the Ten Commandments and on the Our Father were given in the parish church of Wittenberg. Luther's warnings against popular misunderstanding of indulgences also would be better placed in the parish church than in the castle church. An important question yet to be answered is the date of the liturgical celebration of the consecration of the parish church.

But if Luther did after all give this sermon in the castle church, then it was certainly not on October 31, for the feast of the consecration of the castle church was not on All Saints' Day. The document granting the indulgences to be gained in

[4] "Das Entstehungsjahr von Luthers Sermo de indulgentiis pridie Dedicationis," *Zeitschrift für Kirchengeschichte*, XLIII (1924), pp. 174–9.

the castle church lists explicitly these days for gaining indulgences there: All Saints, John the Baptist, St. Vitus, St. Kilian, and the day of the church's dedication.[5] Thus, All Saints' Day and the dedication day are distinct. Cardinal Peraudi had in fact consecrated the castle church in late December 1502. Such a date would not have been convenient for the annual feast of the consecration, and as was customary the feast would have been transferred.[6]

One possible date for the sermon—in the castle church—would be the second Sunday after Easter or the following Monday which is mentioned in the records as the day of a full exposition of the relics of the castle church.[7] In 1517, this Monday fell on April 26,[8] a date which would fit well with Tetzel's movements, since he had been in Jüterbog on April 10, 1517, when people from Wittenberg raced over "like men possessed" to hear his sermons. However, as we said, Luther may well have given the sermon in the parish church and thus have intended no reference to the exposition of relics. One sentence of the sermon says, "Since this pomp of indulgences is before the doors. . . ." (W 1, 98, 18) Here, though, "*prae foribus*" is not a reference to an exposition of relics but to Tetzel's sermons in Jüterbog, a city close enough to be considered as before the city gates of Wittenberg. The sermon, furthermore, makes explicit reference to a papal bull. However the bull which confirmed the indulgences granted to the castle church by Cardinal Peraudi was not issued to Prince Frederick until 1519. Also it is probable that Luther's bitter polemic

[5] P. Kalkoff, *Ablass- und Reliquienverehrung an der Schlosskirche zu Wittenberg* (Gotha: 1907), p. 9; and *Forschungen zu Luthers römischem Prozess* (Rome: 1905), p. 185.

[6] A. Tibus treats the question of transferring the commemoration of the dedication of a church: "Wann ist der Dom zu Münster konskriert worden?" *Westfälische Zeitschrift*, XXIV (1864), pp. 337–60. See also A. Schröer, "Die Münsterer Domweihe (1246)," *Monasterium-Festschrift zum 700jährigen Weihegedächtnis des Domes zu Münster* (Münster: 1966), p. 122f.

[7] Kalkoff, *Ablass und Reliquienverehrung an der Schlosskirche zu Wittenberg*, pp. 47, 52, 96, 107f.

[8] H. Barge, *Andreas Bodenstein von Karlstadt* (Leipzig: 1905), I, 463.

against indulgence preachers was directed against traveling preachers such as Tetzel, since it was Luther and his fellow priests in Wittenberg who were responsible for preaching on indulgences in the castle church. In criticizing his colleagues Luther would have been more restrained and would have avoided such terms as "*seductores*" and "*fabulatores*." (W 1, 98, 15)

Luther begins from the gospel pericope of the feast. (Luke 19:1–10) The passage shows two ways of seeking Christ: Some come to him just to have their own justice confirmed, while others, like Zacchaeus, feel so unworthy that they dare not approach him. The latter, though, are precisely the ones he seeks out. "For he cannot come to those who judge themselves just and worthy, but only to the needy people who see themselves as unworthy of grace and who long for mercy." (W 1, 97, 25f.)

But indulgence preachers promote self-righteousness instead of bringing people to the humble self-knowledge Zacchaeus had. Luther did not want to say much on the topic of indulgences, for he had already spoken about them on another occasion, when the great pomp of indulgences was at the doors.[9] Still, he does not want to implicate himself in any guilt by neglecting his pastoral duty and letting his hearers be led into misunderstanding. Luther protests solemnly that the pope's intention is correct, at least in the strict wording of the bull. In fact, what the preachers are so loudly proclaiming is not wholly false, although it gives rise to misunderstanding.

Luther declares that there are two kinds of penance: "sign penance" and real penance. The latter is the interior and genuine penance about which Christ spoke in Matt. 4:17. Sign penance is external, having confession and satisfaction as its parts. However, Luther finds scripture speaking only of public confession (Jas. 5:16) and of a lifelong satisfaction.

[9] "Dixi enim de iis alias plura, maxime cum sit prae foribus pompa ista indulgentiarum, Ut sim ego excusatus et vos a periculo falsae intelligentiae eruamini" W 1, 98, 17ff.

(Luke 3:8) The jurists should try to work out a proof that confession and satisfaction as now practiced are of divine law.

Indulgences should help promote true, interior penance, but in themselves they only free from privately imposed punishments.[10] Often Luther fears indulgences hinder interior penance, since a penitent who is sincerely displeased with himself and is turning to God with a heartfelt admission of his sins will want to be punished instead of being freed from penance through indulgences. Indulgences are too easily connected with "gallows sorrow," i.e., the fear of punishment and love of self that fundamentally hates God's justice and perversely loves one's own sins. True penance, however, rests on love of justice and expresses itself in hatred of sin and in the will to repair God's offended justice. He concludes, "So you see how dangerous this indulgence preaching is . . . which teaches men to flee satisfaction and punishments." (W 1, 99, 20f.)

Thus, it is not the case that Luther simply rejects indulgences. Rather, he wants to stress, as he does in the ninety-five theses, that indulgences are not connected with the interior and genuine penance Christ preached (Matt. 4:17) nor with the satisfaction mentioned in Luke 3:8. Both of these are for all Christians and are lifelong tasks.[11] Indulgences are valid only regarding the satisfaction imposed in private, sacramental confession. Since they are essentially a mitigation of penance, Luther believes that a true penitent would seek no indulgences and no remittance of his penance. (See W 4, 674, 26ff.)

Luther was not the first to speak of indulgences as an alleviation granted to people who were not zealous for penance. Nor was he the first to point out the danger that proliferation of indulgences could sap the spirit of penance

[10] "*. . . tollunt autem nihil aliud quam privatae satisfactionis impositiones.*" W 1, 98, 38. In the other version: "Ceterum indulgentiae prerequirunt contritionis veritatem, prodesse autem possunt tantum ad privatae confessionis satisfactionem." W 4, 674, 24.

[11] "*. . . est totius vitae Christianae officium et generalis omnibus imposita et publica.*" W 1, 98, 34; 4, 674, 22.

and even open the way to further sin. In 1414 the faculty of Oxford University had called attention to this danger, and at the Council of Constance a complaint was made about the multiplication of indulgences.[12]

The chronicle of the Benedictine, Nikolaus von Siegen, tells about misgivings expressed when the cardinal-legate, Peraudi, preached an indulgence in Erfurt in 1488. The confessional letters were thought to be leading souls into danger and a widely known preacher remarked, "Now laymen and priests living in concubinage say to themselves, 'Now we'll have a real go at sinning, since we can be so easily absolved.' "[13]

Johannes von Paltz, an Erfurt Augustinian, reported that some people boasted of being able to reach heaven merely on the strength of a confessional letter—without contrition or confession.[14]

Thus, Luther's sermon was by no means extraordinary in content or in the sharpness of its criticism of indulgences as a flight from penance and satisfaction. (W 4, 674, 30) And this last point is especially clear evidence that this sermon was given on a date near October 31, 1517.

In a later remark at table Luther told how he had countered the "infamous words" of the indulgence preachers by warning the people against indulgences. At the same time he made intensive studies in order to clarify for himself the very sketchy doctrinal basis of indulgences. (WTr 5, 77, n. 5349) The sermons we have treated show Luther warning the people, and a short treatise on indulgences was the fruit of his study. This treatise was edited by V. E. Löscher in 1720 as a sermon given on the tenth Sunday after Trinity, July 27, 1516, and published under the title: "*Ex sermone habito Dom. X. post Trinit. A. 1516 27 Juli.*" (W 1, 65) However, another version

[12] Paulus, *Geschichte des Ablasses im Mittelalter*, III, 156f.

[13] Nikolaus von Siegen, "*Chronicon Ecclesiasticum*," edited by F. X. Wegele, in *Thüringische Geschichtsquellen* (Jena: 1885), II, 479. See also Paulus, *Johann Tetzel*, p. 126.

[14] Paulus, *Johann Tetzel*, p. 99.

of the same writing was found among copies of Archbishop Albrecht's December 1517 correspondence with the faculty of Mainz University under the title "*Tractatus de Indulgentiis per Doctorem Martinum ordinis S. Augustini Wittenbergae editus.*"[15]

Thus, this is the treatise that Luther sent to Archbishop Albrecht with his ninety-five theses, and which Albrecht mentioned no less than three times in his letter to his Magdeburg councillors on December 13, 1517.[16] Luther himself refers to the treatise in his *Resolutiones* on thesis 26, where he treats the ways in which the pope can make disposition of the *thesaurus* of the church militant: "As I both taught and wrote earlier, the pope has in his power three ways of applying the merits of the church militant: first, that he offer it to God as satisfaction for others; second, as intercession for the departed; and third, to glorify God." (W 1, 580, 11ff.) In the treatise on indulgences Luther divided the last section according to this threefold distinction.[17] The words "*et docui et scripsi*" in the resolution indicate that the indulgence doctrine of the treatise is Luther's own position. This contrasts with Luther's views in the ninety-five theses. For we must take seriously Luther's frequent protestations that in the theses he often asserted points that were quite doubtful in order to stimulate discussion.[18]

Luther begins his treatise by mentioning the sad contrast between the matter itself, a question of the merits of Christ and the saints, which calls for great reverence, and the avarice of

[15] F. Herrmann, "Luthers Tractatus de indulgentiis," *Zeitschrift für Kirchengeschichte*, XXVIII (1907), pp. 370–3; and G. Krüger, "Luthers Tractatus de Indulgentiis," *Theologische Studien und Kritiken*, XC (1917), pp. 507–12. Krüger gives an improved text of Luther's treatise, *Ibid.*, pp. 514–26, which Köhler took over in the second edition of his *Dokumente zum Ablassstreit von 1517*, pp. 94–9. Köhler though still referred to this text as a sermon given in 1516. See also Volz, *Martin Luthers Thesenanschlag*, p. 84, n. 70; and "Erzbischof Albrecht von Mainz und Martin Luthers 95 Thesen," *Jahrbuch der Hessischen kirchengeschichtlichen Vereinigung*, XIII (1962), p. 221, n. 129.

[16] Herrmann, "Luthers Tractatus de indulgentiis," p. 370.

[17] Köhler, *Dokumente*, p. 97, l. 29 to p. 99, l. 24. All references to the *Tractatus* are to Köhler's edition.

[18] For example in WBr 1, 139, 52; 152, 11; 170, 42; and W 1, 528, 38.

those administering indulgences. They have no care for the salvation of souls but only want to fill their purses. They give no instruction on what an indulgence is, and consequently the people think they can gain immediate salvation through indulgences.[19]

In themselves (*saltem per se*) indulgences do not grant the grace of justification nor increase it. Instead they only remit punishments and imposed satisfactions. This remission does not mean that after gaining an indulgence one who dies is certain of going straight to heaven.[20]

In his *Lectures on Romans* (1515–16) Luther had attacked scholastic theologians for not distinguishing between forgiveness (*remissio*) of sin and expulsion (*ablatio*) of sin. (W 56, 273, 3–274, 11) In the indulgence treatise he again underscores how the people have been led astray on this point. They think that forgiveness expels sin totally, and consequently they go on sinning merrily, binding themselves all the more with concupiscence.[21]

In justification, the remission of actual sins does not mean that the sinful habits, i.e., concupiscence, stemming from original sin and from personal sin are expelled. Rather, these are removed only after a long process with the help of God's grace. Therefore, an indulgence does not simply mean that a person is ready for heaven. To be prepared for heaven a twofold grace is necessary: a grace of forgiveness and a grace of infusion, an external and an internal grace.[22] The grace of

[19] "*. . . ut credat se statim salvum adeptis istis indulgentiis.*" Köhler, *Dokumente*, p. 94, ll. 21f.

[20] "Non enim ea gratia ibi confertur, saltem per se, qua quis iustus aut iustior fiat, sed tantum remissio poenitentiae et satisfactionis iniunctae, qua dimissa non sequitur, quod statim evolet in coelum." *Ibid.*, p. 94, l. 22.

[21] "Stultus autem et maior pars populi decepta credit per plenariam remissionem ita peccatum omne auferri, ut statim evolet, et strenue peccat et aggravat se vinculis concupiscentiae." *Ibid.*, p. 94, l. 26. As we saw above, the "*Instructio summaria*" described the first principal grace of the indulgence as the full remission of sins and the complete removal of the punishments of purgatory.

[22] "Unde notandum, quod duplex est gratia, scilicet remissionis et infusionis, seu extrinseca et intrinseca." Köhler, *Dokumente*, p. 94, ll. 30f.

forgiveness (an indulgence) is the remission of penances which have been imposed by a confessor to be performed on earth or endured in purgatory. This remission does not however increase our charity nor diminish our concupiscence. And concupiscence must be extinguished before one enters God's kingdom. These latter effects stem from the infused grace that illumines our mind and inflames our will. This grace is given to those who confess their sins in perfect sorrow. The complete extinction of concupiscence is shown by a sigh of longing for God and of disgust for this life leading to the dissolution of one's earthly body. But such a desire for God is very seldom present among those gaining indulgences. Therefore it is extremely dangerous to preach that a plenary indulgence frees a soul from purgatory.

Now the pope's power of the keys does not extend to purgatory nor to the granting of this infused grace that expels concupiscence. If it did, then the pope would be cruel if he did not grant the poor souls freely what he grants them for someone's contribution to the church. Instead, the pope can only apply the intercession of the whole church in petition for this interior grace.[23]

Thus, the church has two ways of helping penitents: with the power of the keys the church remits the penances that have been imposed and by way of intercession begs God for healing grace to expel concupiscence. The extent to which this intercession is successful is uncertain, since it depends on God's acceptance of the church's prayer. Another factor causing uncertainty is that no one knows if he has the perfect contrition required for gaining an indulgence in the first place. The effectiveness of the church's intercession for a departed soul is also dependent, as Augustine taught,[24] on the extent to which the person made himself worthy of help

[23] "Nec hoc papa habet solvere ullo modo per auctoritatem clavis, sed solummodo per applicationem intercessionis totius ecclesiae, ubi adhuc dubium remanet, pro quanto, an pro toto deus hoc velit acceptare." *Ibid.*, p. 95, l. 8.

[24] Denzinger-Schönmetzer, *Enchiridion Symbolorum*, 29 (110); PL 40, 283.

during his earthly life through contrition and detachment from this world.

Luther then raises an objection which he admittedly cannot satisfactorily answer: what function do indulgences have, since one in perfect contrition comes to heaven without their help, and one with imperfect contrition cannot enter heaven no matter how many indulgences he has? From this point Luther attacks the contemporary theology of sin as being superficial in attending only to sinful deeds and not to the root sin that remains.[25]

Luther then offers this possible explanation: perhaps an indulgence which by the power of the keys remits imposed penances can also, *per modum suffragii*, gain from God the grace of perfect contrition, love of God, and heartfelt longing for God.[26] For instance, if a person dies unresigned to death and still attached to this world, then it is clear that he dies in sin although not in mortal sin. His own powers are not sufficient to free him from this attachment, nor is the fire of purgatory an apt means for bringing this about. What he needs is grace, and it could well be that the intercession of the church gains for him the grace of repentance so that he becomes willingly resigned to death. In this way indulgences, as intercessory prayers of the church for the departed, can contribute to the interior cleansing from the root sin of concupiscence.

At this point, Luther proposes that all the merits of Christ and of the saints are in the hands of the pope and can be applied in three different ways. He speaks of "all the good that Christ brings about in the church" and explains that this can be applied as satisfaction, as intercession, or as a sacrifice of praise. The application as satisfaction is for the living, who through indulgences gain remittance of punishments for ac-

[25] "*. . . de fomitis mortificatione et radicali peccato amplius nemo est sollicitus; tantum de actualibus curant amputandis.*" Köhler, *Dokumente*, p. 97, ll. 4f.

[26] "An forte per hoc, quod dicunt 'per modum suffragii,' quod illud suffragium non tantum atualium eis remissionem conferat, sed etiam contritionem et poenitentiam super fomite et reliquiis amoris terreni impetret ac gratiam perfectissimi amoris dei ac suspirium ad deum conferat?" *Ibid.*, ll. 11ff.

tual sins. This remission is however no ground for security since the roots of sin are still to be extinguished. For eradication of these roots one must apply himself to mortification, or else concupiscence will lead to further sins.

By way of intercession, the pope can apply the spiritual goods of the church through an indulgence for the departed. He cannot absolve the dead but can only beg God to free them from the punishments for actual sins and from the roots of sin not yet expelled in this life. We should not speak lightly about the effects of this intercession, since we do not know how this soul stands before God. Nonetheless, the pope can do more for the departed than he can do for the living, since he only grants the latter a remission of punishments, but he can gain for the dead the infused grace of inner, personal renewal.[27]

About the effect of an indulgence there can be no absolute certitude, since God must freely decide whether and to what extent he answers the prayer of his church. But God will hardly refuse prayer since Christ himself prays in and with the church. Thus, in spite of the abuses stemming from the avarice and commercial spirit of the indulgence preachers, Luther still saw indulgences as useful. Even their multiplication in his time appears fitting. For Christians had grown spiritually tepid, with the result that more of them were going to purgatory than previously, and fewer were praying for these souls.[28] It was only right that the pope come to their aid. On the third manner in which the pope applies the goods of the church—in praise of God—Luther had nothing more to say. This suggests that he took over the threefold division from someone else.

We can summarize Luther's conception of indulgences as follows: an indulgence is a remission which frees one from the

[27] "Unde plus videtur papa facere cum indulgentiis pro defunctis quam pro vivis, quia et gratiam infusionis eis impetrat, vivis autem solam remissionem concedit." *Ibid.*, p. 98, ll. 32ff.

[28] Biel made a similar point, *Canonis Misse Expositio*, *lectio* 57 O, Oberman-Courtenay ed., II, 408.

satisfaction imposed by the confessor (*remissio . . . iniunctae satisfactionis*).[29] As such it removes the penance which the church had imposed to be undergone in this life or in purgatory. An indulgence does not lessen concupiscence nor does it bring an increase of grace and charity.

Luther's aim was to cause people to be concerned about genuine penance, i.e., about personal conversion, the expulsion of the roots of sin, and growth in interior virtue.[30] An indulgence is not an exemption from this work of penance, a point Luther stressed in the first of his ninety-five theses. Therefore, if indulgences inculcate false security and spiritual inertia, if they distract men from remedying concupiscence and longing for God, they are to be rejected. Luther's treatise closes: "Let us constantly seek God's healing grace."[31]

The starting point of Luther's argumentation was the religious practice of his times, with its externalized understanding of satisfaction, even to the point where penance could be simply remitted in return for a contribution of money. Luther however did not direct his words to this basic point in striving to make people more aware of the work of healing or of the inner conversion that should be the ground for sacramental satisfaction. Instead, he simply posited an externalized understanding of satisfaction and proceeded to separate completely the penance imposed by the church in confession from the penance imposed by God for interior healing. The former—satisfactory penance—can be remitted by an indulgence; the latter—healing penance—can be remitted only through contrition, or in the case of the souls in purgatory, by the application *per modum suffragii* of the merits of the church.

[29] Köhler, *Dokumente*, p. 94, l. 24.

[30] "Sed per hanc [gratiam remissionis extrinsecae] nihil minuitur concupiscentia et morbus naturae nec augetur dilectio nec ulla gratia aut virtus interior, quae tamen omnia fieri oportet, antequam regnum dei intrent." *Ibid.*, p. 95, ll. 2ff.

[31] ". . . *assidue sanantem gratiam eius quaeramus.*" *Ibid.*, p. 99, ll. 30f.

Philipp Melanchthon, from an engraving by Albrecht Dürer

The "*Summma angelica*"[32] had also distinguished between the increase of grace and the remission of punishment through indulgences. Indulgences grant an increase of grace and glory in strict correspondence with the disposition of the recipient. But the extent of punishment remitted is that named in the indulgence itself. The effect of an indulgence is independent of the recipient's disposition, provided that he fulfill the set conditions. Luther went beyond the "*Summa angelica*" by completely excluding the idea of an increase of grace through an indulgence. In the resolution given for the twentieth of his ninety-five theses he argued for this from the position that an indulgence was not precisely a good work but rather the commutation of a good work for a lesser work.[33]

Late medieval theology and practice had destroyed the sign value of ecclesiastical penance and indulgences by practically identifying them with what was signified, i.e., the remission before God of punishment for sin. Luther was, however, in danger of doing the same by denying any connection between the sign and the thing signified, and by maintaining that ecclesial-sacramental penance had no relevance for remission of punishments before God.

[32] See p. 12, n. 21, above. In the explanation of his twentieth indulgence thesis Luther spoke twice explicitly of the "*Summa angelica*" (W. 1, 568, 4; 569, 41). Luther borrows from the "*Summa angelica*" in his description of the various opinions on how an indulgence attains its effect. The "*Summa angelica*" had given seven opinions, and favored the seventh: ". . . indulgentia quantum ad augmentum gratiae et gloriae tantum valet quantum est interna devotio suscipientis et non plus: quantum vero ad remissionem poenae debitae in purgatorio vel impositae a sacerdote in paenitentia, dico quod indulgentia tantum dimittit quantum sonat . . . dummodo hoc faciat, quod sibi imponitur." s.v. "*Indulgentia*," chap. 2. In his explanations, on W 1, 567, 36 and 575, 22ff., Luther also alludes to this sentence of the "*Summa angelica*" on a plenary indulgence: "Aliquando simpliciter datur remissio omnium peccatorum: et tunc si nullum peccatum post comiserit statim evolaret ad gloriam si moreretur." See also the treatment of this question of immediate entry into heaven when one dies after gaining a plenary indulgence by Johannes von Paltz in his *Coelifodina*, Köhler, *Dokumente*, pp. 81ff.

[33] "Porro id quod Angelus ex suo Francisco Maronis adducit, quod indulgentiae etiam valent ad augmentum gratiae et gloriae. Non advertit quod indulgentiae non sunt opera bona, sed remissiones bonorum operum propter aliud minus opus." W 1, 570, 2ff.

We must respect the earnestness with which Luther struggled in his treatise with a theological problem that even to our own day has not been wholly solved. What a momentous consequence it was that instead of this balanced treatise it was Luther's polemical disputation on indulgences which became influential in the following months.

IV. LUTHER WRITES TO THE BISHOPS

LUTHER THOUGHT for a time that the ideas about indulgences which he found objectionable were private opinions held and disseminated by the preachers. He thought the abuses of the indulgences arose from commercialized preaching. He had stressed that the papal bull was itself quite correct (W 1, 98, 19f.) and had even cited the bull in support of his own delimitation of the power of the keys.[1] He related that he knew nothing at first about Albrecht's negotiations with the curia and that he had not seen the "*Instructio summaria.*" When however a copy of the *instructio* came into his hands it became clear that Tetzel's preaching was to some extent based on official instructions.

Let us hear Luther's own narrative of 1541 from *Wider Hans Worst:*

> This same Tetzel now went around with indulgences, selling grace for money as dearly or cheaply as he could, to the best of his ability. At that time I was a preacher here in the monastery, and a fledgling doctor, fervent and enthusiastic for holy scripture.
>
> Now when many people from Wittenberg went to Jüterbog and Zerbst for indulgences, and I (as truly as my Lord Christ redeemed me) did not know what the indulgences were, as in fact no one knew, I began to preach very gently that one could probably do something better and more reliable than acquire indulgences. I had also preached before in the same way against indulgences at the castle and had thus gained the disfavor of Duke Frederick because he was very fond of his religious founda-

[1] "Sicut sonat eius bulla: 'In quantum claves sanctae matris ecclesiae se extendunt.' " Köhler, *Dokumente*, p. 95, l. 13.

tion. Now I—to point out the true cause of the Lutheran rumpus—let everything take its course. However I heard what dreadful and abominable articles Tetzel was preaching, and some of them I shall mention now, namely:

That he had such grace and power from the pope that even if someone seduced the holy Virgin Mary, and made her conceive, he could forgive him, provided he placed the necessary sum in the box.

Again, that the red indulgence cross, bearing the papal arms, was when erected in church as powerful as the cross of Christ.

Again, that if St. Peter were here now, he would not have greater grace or power than he had.

Again, that he would not change places with St. Peter in heaven, for he had rescued more souls with indulgences than St. Peter had with his preaching.

Again, that if anyone put money in the box for a soul in purgatory, the soul would fly to heaven as soon as the coin clinked on the bottom of the box.

Again, that the grace from indulgences was the same grace as that by which a man is reconciled to God.

Again, that it was not necessary to have remorse, sorrow, or repentance for sin, if one bought (I ought to say, acquired) an indulgence or a dispensation; indeed he sold also for future sin.

He did an abominable amount of this, and it was all for the sake of money. I did not know at that time who would get the money. Then a booklet appeared, magnificently ornamented with the coat of arms of the bishop of Magdeburg, in which the sellers of indulgences were advised to preach some of these articles. It became quite evident that Bishop Albrecht had hired this Tetzel because he was a great ranter; for he was elected bishop of Mainz with the agreement that he was himself to buy (I mean acquire) the pallium at Rome. For three bishops of Mainz—Berthold, Jakob, and Uriel—had recently died, one shortly after the other, so that it was perhaps difficult for the diocese to buy the pallium so often and in such quick succession, since it cost twenty-six thousand gulden according to some, and thirty thousand according to others, for the most holy father of Rome can charge as much as that for flax (which otherwise is hardly worth six cents).

Thus the bishop devised this scheme, hoping to pay the Fuggers (for they had advanced the money for the pallium) from the purse of the common man. And he sent this great fleecer of men's pockets into the provinces; he fleeced them so thoroughly that a pile of money began to come clinking and clattering into the boxes. He did not forget himself in this either. And in addition the pope had a finger in the pie as well, because one-half was to go toward building St. Peter's Church in Rome. Thus these fellows went about their work joyfully and full of hope, rattling their boxes under men's purses and fleecing them. But, as I say, I did not know that at the time.

Then I wrote a letter with the *Theses* to the bishop of Magdeburg, admonishing and beseeching him to stop Tetzel and prevent this stupid thing from being preached, lest it give rise to public discontent—that was the proper thing for him to do as archbishop. I can still lay my hands on that letter.[2]

This letter, of which Luther could produce a copy in 1541, was first printed in the first volume of his Latin works in Wittenberg in 1545.[3] The original of the letter is extant in the Swedish royal archives in Stockholm.[4] This letter to Archbishop Albrecht bears the date of October 31, 1517, and is important enough to be quoted in full.

Jesus. Grace and mercy from God and my complete devotion. Most Reverend Father in Christ, Most Illustrious Sovereign: Forgive me that I, the least of all men, have the temerity to consider writing to Your Highness. The Lord Jesus is my witness that I have long hesitated doing this on account of my insignificance and unworthiness, of which I am well aware. I do it now impudently, and I am motivated solely by the obligation of my loyalty, which I know I owe you, Most Reverend Father in Christ. May Your Highness therefore deign to glance at what is but a grain of dust and, for the sake of your episcopal kindness, listen to my request.

Under your most distinguished name, papal indulgences are

[2] W 51, 538, 29–540, 19. LW 41, 231–3 (Eric W. Gritsch).

[3] Volz, *Martin Luthers Thesenanschlag*, p. 85, n. 73.

[4] According to Volz (*Ibid.*, p. 87, n. 87) the letter is reproduced in *Kyrkohistorik Arsskrift*, XVIII (1917), pp. 34ff. See also the facsimiles given by Volz, pp. 32f., illus. nn. 3, 4.

offered all across the land for the construction of St. Peter. Now, I do not so much complain about the quacking of the preachers, which I haven't heard; but I bewail the gross misunderstanding among the people which comes from these preachers and which they spread everywhere among common men. Evidently the poor souls believe that when they have bought indulgence letters they are then assured of their salvation.[5] They are likewise convinced that souls escape from purgatory as soon as they have placed a contribution into the chest.[6] Further, they assume that the grace obtained through these indulgences is so completely effective that there is no sin of such magnitude that it cannot be forgiven—even if (as they say) someone should rape the Mother of God, were this possible.[7] Finally they also believe that man is freed from every penalty and guilt by these indulgences.[8]

O great God! The souls committed to your care, excellent Father, are thus directed to death. For all these souls you have the heaviest and a constantly increasing responsibility. Therefore I can no longer be silent on this subject. No man can be assured of his salvation by any episcopal function. He is not even assured of his salvation by the infusion of God's grace, because the Apostle orders us to work out our salvation constantly "in fear and trembling." Even "the just will hardly be saved." Finally the way that leads to life is so narrow that the Lord, through the prophets Amos and Zechariah, calls those that will be saved "a brand plucked out of the fire." And everywhere else the Lord proclaims the difficulty of salvation. How can they [indulgence agents] then make the people feel secure and without fear [concerning salvation] by means of those false stories and promises of pardon?[9] After all, the indulgences contribute absolutely nothing to the salvation and holiness of souls; they only compensate for the external punishment which—on the basis of canon law—once used to be imposed.[10]

[5] See Luther's ninety-five theses, Thesis 32.

[6] See Thesis 27. See also W 30II, 284, 21f.

[7] See Theses 75 and 76. Tetzel called this version of his preaching calumnious in his protests of December 12 and 14, 1517. V. Gröne, *Tetzel und Luther* (Soest: 1860), pp. 234–7. On Thesis 76, see W 30II, 284, 18ff.

[8] See Theses 21 and 76. See also W 30II, 282, 15.

[9] See Theses 77 and 79 for examples of these promises.

[10] See Thesis 5.

Works of piety and love are infinitely better than indulgences;[11] and yet [the indulgence preachers] do not preach them with an equally big display and effort. What is even worse, [the preachers] are silent about them because they have to preach the sale of the indulgences. The first and only duty of the bishops, however, is to see that the people learn the gospel and the love of Christ. For on no occasion has Christ ordered that indulgences should be preached, but he forcefully commanded the gospel to be preached. What a horror, what a danger for a bishop to permit the loud noise of indulgences among his people, while the gospel is silenced, and to be more concerned with the sale of indulgences than with the gospel![12] Will not Christ say to [such bishops], "You strain out a gnat but swallow a camel"?

Added to all this, my Most Reverend Father in the Lord, is the fact that in the *Instruction* for the indulgence agents which is published under Your Highness' name, it is written (certainly without your full awareness and consent, Most Reverend Father) that one of the principal graces [bestowed through the indulgences] is that inestimable gift of God by which a man is reconciled with God and by which all the punishments of purgatory are blotted out.[13] It also is written there that contrition is not necessary on the part of those who buy off their souls or acquire *confessionalia*.[14]

What can I do, excellent Bishop and Most Illustrious Sovereign? I can only beg you, Most Reverend Father, through the Lord Jesus Christ, to deign to give this matter your fatherly attention and totally withdraw that little book and command the preachers of indulgences to preach in another way. If this is not done, someone may rise and, by means of publications, silence those preachers and refute your little book. This would be the greatest disgrace for Your Most Illustrious Highness. I

[11] See Theses 43 and 44. Compare Biel (*Canonis Missae Expositio, lectio* 57 Q, Oberman-Courtenay ed., II, 409) with Luther's marginal note (*Luthers Randbemerkungen zu G. Biels Collectorium und Canonis Missae Expositio*, edited by H. Degering [Weimar: 1933], p. 19).

[12] See Theses 53–5, and W 30II, 282, 23f.

[13] This is found almost literally in the "*Instructio summaria*," Köhler, *Dokumente*, p. 110, ll. 24ff.

[14] "*Instructio summaria*," *Ibid.*, p. 116, ll. 1, 25. See Luther's Thesis 33, and W 30II, 284, 23.

certainly shudder at this possibility, yet I am afraid it will happen if things are not quickly remedied.

I beg your Most Illustrious Grace to accept this faithful service of my humble self in a princely and episcopal—that is, in the most kind—way, just as I am rendering it with a most honest heart, and in absolute loyalty to you, Most Reverend Father. For I too am a part of your flock. May the Lord Jesus protect you, Most Reverend Father, forever. Amen.

From Wittenberg, 1517. All Saints' Eve.

Were it agreeable to your Most Reverend Father, you could examine my disputation theses, so that you may see how dubious is this belief concerning indulgences, which these preachers propagate as if it were the surest thing in the whole world.

Your unworthy son
Martin Luther,
Augustinian,
called Doctor of Sacred Theology[15]

Thus Luther begged the archbishop to withdraw the "*Instructio summaria*" and to issue new directives to the preachers. His complaint is not based directly upon the words of Tetzel or of other preachers. He admits that he had not heard them. Instead, he begins from the erroneous ideas and hopes stirred up in those who heard the sermons.[16]

Specifically, there were four popular misunderstandings that Luther brought to the archbishop's attention:

1. An indulgence makes salvation certain.
2. With the gift of money, a soul goes immediately to heaven.
3. Through the grace of this indulgence, the worst imaginable sins can be forgiven.
4. An indulgence frees from all guilt and punishment.

[15] WBr 1, 110–2. LW 48, 45–9 (G. G. Krodel).

[16] In the explanation of Thesis 32, Luther wrote not without irony, "I am not censuring anyone, for I should not do so since I have not heard the indulgence preachers. As far as I am concerned, they may excuse themselves until they become whiter than snow. Surely these people must be reproved for having wax in their ears so that they hear only pernicious things when these preachers tell them salutary things." W 1, 587, 32ff. LW 31, 180 (Carl M. Folkemer).

Luther's first point takes up a theme stressed throughout his early works. As early as 1513–15, in the "*Dictata super Psalterium*," Luther's first major lecture course, he had warned against false security. In fact, he followed St. Bernard of Clairvaux in pointing to *pax et securitas* as the specific temptation threatening the church in his own age, after successful vanquishment of the trials of persecution and heresy.[17]

In the *Lectures on Romans*, 1515–16, Luther sought to counter the deadly temptation to false security by stressing, again with Bernard, that in Christian living to stand still is to fall back:

> Therefore the whole life of the new people, the people of faith and of the spirit, consists in the sigh of the heart, the cry of deeds, and the work of the body by which they desire, seek, and petition ever to be further justified until death. They never stand still, thinking they are at their goal.[18]

Luther's other three points of complaint in the letter to Albrecht are criticisms of the "*Instructio summaria*," which had at least lent support to such misunderstanding and exaggeration.[19]

Luther can call this a "deadly" instruction for the people, since it makes no mention of how narrow the way to salvation actually is. Even infused divine grace, to say nothing of an indulgence, does not make salvation absolutely certain. Luther underscores the great responsibility of the bishops in this situation. He makes only a brief statement of his own conception of indulgences. His one sentence, though, is clearly connected with his ninety-five theses. That he speaks so succinctly in his letter is an indication that he is sure of his position: ". . . indulgences contribute absolutely nothing to the salvation and holiness of souls; they only compensate for the

[17] "Ut Bernardus ait: quae fuit amara sub tyrannis, amarior sub haereticis, amarissima sub pacificis et securis." W 3, 417, 7f.

[18] W 56, 264, 16ff.

[19] See above, p. 20f.

external punishment which—on the basis of canon law—once used to be imposed."[20]

In his letter Luther stressed the bishop's pastoral responsibilities. A bishop's first duty is the proclamation of the gospel. What a disgrace and what a danger for a bishop who supports the noisy promotion of indulgences while neglecting the gospel. Luther begged the archbishop to withdraw the *instructio* and to issue new directives for the preachers. He made this entreaty more emphatic by pointing to the danger that someone might write against the preachers and against the *instructio* in a manner detrimental to the good name and authority of the archbishop. We cannot be certain whether this was a vague warning or whether Luther was already thinking of taking such a step himself. If so, Luther would be presenting Albrecht with an ultimatum, which he then strengthened considerably by sending his ninety-five theses along with the letter. This interpretation of Luther's words is supported by a later remark in the *Table Talk:*

> The monstrosities of Tetzel's preaching on indulgences moved me to oppose him. I sought no fame or profit, but first fell prostrate before God and begged his support. At that time I saw only a few of the worst abuses, and had no idea that these abominations came from the pope himself. Therefore I wrote suppliantly to the bishops of Brandenburg and Mainz, saying that if they did not suppress this evil I would write against it. But the bishops sent my letter to Tetzel.[21]

After dating the letter "*Vigilia omnium sanctorum*," but before signing it, Luther added the postscript to call Albrecht's attention to the enclosed disputation theses. These were to show the archibishop how problematic was the indulgence doctrine which the preachers gave out as absolutely certain.[22]

[20] "Indulgentiae prorsus nihil boni conferant animabus ad salutem aut sanctitatem, sed tantummodo poenam externam, olim canonice imponi solitam, auferant." WBr 1, 111, 34ff.

[21] WTr 5, 657, n. 6431.

[22] "Si t[uae] reverendissimae p[aternitati] placet, poterit has meas disputationes videre, ut intelligat, quam dubia res sit indulgentiarum opinio, quam illi ut certissimam seminant." WBr 1, 112, 66ff.

The date of the letter, October 31, does not tell us exactly when Luther wrote his ninety-five theses. They may have been written beforehand, or they could even have been written later. It is clearly possible that the letter to the archbishop lay on Luther's desk for a few days and that Luther's impatient concern for his topic spurred him to write the theses in the first days of November. In this case, Luther's threat of a written attack would have been partially realized already, and the ultimatum would pertain to the publication of the theses. This hypothesis that the theses were written after composition of the letter would perhaps make more intelligible the sequence of dating the letter, the reference to the theses, and the signature following the suggestion that Albrecht examine the theses. Furthermore, it conforms better with a table remark in which Luther told of a walk he took with Hieronymus Schurff after All Saints' Day in 1517, and of Schurff's startled reaction when Luther told him of his intention to write against the errors held on indulgences.[23]

Thus, Luther had two objectives. First, he wanted to persuade the archbishop to withdraw the "*Instructio summaria*" and to do away with the abuses through a new set of directives for preaching. Second, he hoped to stage an academic disputation to clarify the doctrinal basis of indulgences. These two objectives parallel each other, and in pursuing them Luther was intensely committed both as a pastor and as a theologian. The theses serve to illustrate Luther's petition before the archbishop and to underscore its urgency. They attack the indulgence preaching and the underlying *instructio* just as the letter did but more extensively. Perhaps Luther was already hoping to gain the support of ecclesiastical and civil authorities for a public disputation such as that held in Leipzig in 1519. Thus he would reach beyond a strictly academic audience. This does not mean that the ninety-five theses were only a

[23] WTr 3, 564, n. 3722. We give this in full, p. 76, below.

memorandum for the competent church authorities.[24] Clearly, they were directed all along to a disputation of some kind.

Luther most probably sent the letter with the enclosures to the archiepiscopal residence in Halle (Moritzburg). Albrecht however was staying then in his Aschaffenburg residence near Mainz. Thus the letter was opened by Albrecht's Magdeburg councillors on November 17 in Calbe on the Saale, and from there was sent on to Aschaffenburg. We do not know exactly the day on which Luther's letter and the theses came into the archbishop's hands, but it was clearly in November; for on December 1 Albrecht asked the faculty of the university in Mainz to give a judgment on Luther's theses.[25] The faculty sent its report to the archbishop on December 17. On December 13 Albrecht had written to his Magdeburg councillors acknowledging acceptance of their "letter with enclosed treatise and conclusion written by an impudent monk in Wittenberg on the holy enterprise of indulgences and about our subcommissioners." The writings, Albrecht reported, had been read in his presence and he had sent "the treatise, *conclusiones*, and other writings" to the theologians and jurists of the university in Mainz for their judgment. He also reported that he had sent copies of "the articles, position, and treatise" to the pope.[26]

[24] Kurt Aland appears to attribute this interpretation to me in his article in *Geschichte in Wissenschaft und Unterricht*, XVI (1965), pp. 687f. H. Steubing has misconstrued one of my arguments against the theses posting and thereby has me seeing the ninety-five theses as nothing more than a memo for Luther's ecclesiastical superiors with no relation to a disputation. Steubing failed to tell his readers how Luther stressed that his theses went out only when he received no answer from the bishops, and that the bishops are supposed to have known about them before Luther's closest friends learned of the theses. "Hat Luther die 95 Thesen wirklich angeschlagen?" *Kirche in der Zeit*, XX (1965), pp. 447–52.

[25] Herrmann, "Miscellen zur Reformationsgeschichte," *Zeitschrift für Kirchengeschichte*, XXIII (1902), p. 265. Thus, it is incorrect to say that the letter came to Albrecht on December 13, 1517. Aland, *Geschichte in Wissenschaft und Unterricht*, XVI (1965), p. 688.

[26] F. Körner, *Tezel der Ablassprediger* (Frankenberg: 1880), p. 148. Herrmann, "Luthers Tractatus de indulgentiis," *Zeitschrift für Kirchengeschichte*, XXVIII (1907), p. 370.

According to this letter of December 13, 1517, the councillors had forwarded to the archbishop not only Luther's letter and the ninety-five theses (*conclusiones*) but also a treatise, which Albrecht mentions no fewer than three times. We may suppose that this treatise had also come with Luther's letter and that it is the "Treatise on Indulgences" treated above.

Albrecht suggested that his Magdeburg agents begin a *processus inhibitorius* in which Luther would be summoned and under threat of punishment be enjoined from all further attacks on indulgences in sermons, writings, and disputations.[27] The councillors do not appear to have acted upon this advice from Albrecht. But Albrecht himself did forward the documents to the curia in Rome along with a denunciation against Luther.

Luther spoke later about letters to other bishops on the subject of indulgences at this time.[28] But it was especially the letter to Albrecht that he mentioned frequently all through his life. We shall first simply list Luther's statements.

1. In May 1518, Luther wrote as follows in the letter of dedication to Pope Leo X which was printed with the *Resolutiones* of the ninety-five theses:

> I burned with zeal for the honor of Christ, or, as others will have it, the young blood boiled within me. Yet I saw that I was not the proper one to decide or undertake anything in this matter. Therefore I privately warned a number of prelates.

[27] P. Kalkoff, "Zu Luthers römischen Prozess," *Zeitschrift für Kirchengeschichte*, XXXI (1910), p. 50.

[28] Luther repeatedly mentioned his own ordinary, Bishop Hieronymus Schulz of Brandenburg. Another possibility is the Bishop of Merseburg, in whose diocese Tetzel's Leipzig Dominican priory lay. Myconius named him among the four bishops in addition to Albrecht to whom Luther is supposed to have written (see Myconius' report, p. 60, below). At any rate, the bishop of Merseburg did know about the theses before November 27, 1517. For on this day C. Pflug wrote to Duke George of Saxony that the bishop approved of Luther's intervention and would like to see Luther's theses posted all through the land. Gess, ed., *Akten und Briefe zur Kirchenpolitik Herzog Georgs von Sachsen*, (Leipzig: 1905), I, 28f. See also Volz, *Martin Luthers Thesenanschlag*, pp. 88f., and Honselmann, *Urfassung und Drucke der Ablassthesen Martin Luthers* (Paderborn: 1966), p. 121.

Cardinal Albrecht von Mainz und Brandenburg, from an engraving of 1523 by Albrecht Durer in the Staatliche Museum, Berlin

> Some of them listened to me, others derided me, and others answered in different ways. The terror of your Holiness' name and the fear of excommunication were too strong. At length, no other course was open to me but that of a moderate opposition to the indulgence preachers. So I called their doctrines in doubt and proposed a disputation on the question. I issued my theses and invited learned men to dispute them with me, which even my opponents can see clearly in the preface of the disputation theses.[29]

2. On November 21, 1518, Luther wrote to the prince-elector, Frederick the Wise, about the events of a year before in order to counter certain whispered attacks on the prince:

> One thing vexes me greatly, and this is that the legate [Cajetan] should insinuate that I have acted as I have in reliance upon your Electoral Highness. Some have here in our midst calumniously asserted that I undertook the disputation on indulgences at the suggestion and advice of your Grace. But the fact is that not even my closest friends were aware of it, but only the archbishop of Magdeburg, and Hieronymus, the bishop of Brandenburg. For I admonished in private letters these whose office it was to prevent scandal, most humbly and respectfully, before I published my disputation theses. I knew quite well that I should not bring this matter before civil authorities, but first before the bishops. My letter is still extant; it has passed through many hands and bears witness to what I say.[30]

3. In 1541, Luther gave this account in *Wider Hans Worst:*

> Then I wrote a letter with the theses to the bishop of Magdeburg, admonishing and beseeching him to stop Tetzel and prevent this stupid thing from being preached, lest it give rise to

[29] W 1, 528, 18–26. Translation based on that of Margaret A. Currie, *The Letters of Martin Luther* (London: 1908), p. 29.

[30] WBr 1, 244, 354ff. Currie, ed., *Letters*, p. 37. In the original, the central portion of this text reads, ". . . huius disputationis nullus etiam intimorum amicorum fuerit conscius, nisi Reverendissimus Dominus Archiepiscopus Magdeburgensis et Dominus Hieronymus Episcopus Brandenburgensis. Hos enim, sicut intererat eorum ista monstra prohibere, ita privatis literis, antequam disputationem ederem, humiliter et reverenter monui." This letter was called for by the prince-elector, and eventually came to Cardinal Cajetan, as a defense for the prince against suspicions expressed by the cardinal.

public discontent—this was a proper thing for him to do as archbishop. I can still lay my hands on that letter; but I never received an answer. I wrote in the same manner to the bishop of Brandenburg as my ordinary; in him I had a very gracious bishop. He answered that I was attacking the authority of the church and would get myself into trouble. He advised me to leave it alone. I can well imagine that they both thought the pope would be much too powerful for me, a miserable beggar.

So my theses against Tetzel's articles, which you can now see in print, were published. They went throughout the whole of Germany in a fortnight, for the whole world complained about indulgences, and particularly about Tetzel's articles. And because all the bishops were silent and no one wanted to bell the cat (for the masters of heresy, the preaching order, had instilled fear into the whole world with the threat of fire, and Tetzel had bullied a number of priests who had grumbled against his impudent preaching), Luther became famous as a doctor, for at last someone had stood up to fight. I did not want the fame, because (as I have said) I did not myself know what the indulgences were, and the song might prove too high for my voice. This is the first, real, fundamental beginning of the Lutheran rumpus.[31]

4. In 1545, Luther wrote the autobiographical preface to the first volume of his collected Latin works, which included the letter to Albrecht. He related in the preface:

Soon afterward I wrote two letters, one to Albrecht, the archbishop of Mainz, who got half of the money from the indulgences, the pope the other half—something I did not know at the time—the other to the ordinary (as they call them) Hieronymus, the bishop of Brandenburg. I begged them to stop the shameless blasphemy of the quaestors. But the poor little brother was despised. Despised, I published the theses and at the same time a German sermon on indulgences,[32] shortly thereafter also the *Resolutiones*, in which, to the pope's honor, I developed the idea that indulgences should indeed not be condemned, but that good works of love should be preferred to them.[33]

[31] W 51, 540, 15–541, 7. LW 41, 233–4 (Eric W. Gritsch).

[32] This sermon appeared in March 1518 (W 1, 243–6).

[33] W 54, 180, 12ff.; LW 34, 329–30 (L. W. Spitz). The last sentence begins, "*Ego contemptus edidi Disputationis scedulam.*"

5. In March 1539, Luther said this at table:

> As the gospel made its start, I quietly (*sensim*) opposed the shameless Tetzel. Hieronymus, the bishop of Brandenburg, was favorable to me. I also warned him, as our ordinary, that he should look into this matter. I also sent him a handwritten copy of my explanations of the theses before I published them. But no one wanted to restrain Tetzel's rantings, and some even dared to defend him.[34]

6. In an undated remark at table, Luther related how he had threatened the bishops with an attack if they would not take steps to eliminate the abuses connected with indulgences.[35]

7. Also in an undated table remark from the collection of Johann Aurifaber, Luther was reported to have said about himself:

> As he first began to write against indulgences in 1517, he wrote to the bishop of Brandenburg and begged him to restrain Tetzel. But the bishop answered that "I should not start trouble over this, for if I did I would come to grief for meddling in the affairs of the church." The devil himself was using this bishop as his mouthpiece.[36]

The report given in 1541 by Friedrich Myconius in his *History of the Reformation* agrees in all basic points with Luther's presentation. Myconius wrote:

> First, Doctor Martin wrote to four bishops, that is to the bishops of Meissen, of Frankfurt,[37] of Zeitz, and of Merseburg, and after this to Albrecht, the bishop of Mainz. He reminded all of

[34] WTr 4, 316, n. 4446.

[35] Given above, p. 53.

[36] WTr 6, 238, n. 6861.

[37] Since there was no bishop of Frankfurt Volz judged that Myconius must have meant Hieronymus, bishop of Brandenburg. *Martin Luthers Thesenanschlag*, p. 25. Honselmann would take Myconius at his word and see here a reference to the bishop of Lebus, Dietrich von Bülow (1490–1523), who actually maintained his court in Frankfurt on the Oder, the main city of his diocese, and there contributed notably to the growth of the university and to a flourishing group of humanists.

them that by reason of their episcopal office they should see to it that God's name not be abused and reviled and that the common folk not be so lamentably led astray. The bishop of Mainz disdained to answer. The other bishops gave various answers, e.g., saying that they had no power or authority to act on a matter pertaining to the pope. When Doctor Martin Luther saw that the bishops could not be stirred to act, he wrote various *propositiones* on indulgences, which begin, "*Dominus et Magister noster Christus dicens: Poenitentiam agite, voluit omnem omnium hominum vitam esse poenitentiam.*" He had these printed so that he could hold a disputation among the learned men of the university in Wittenberg to clarify what an indulgence was, what it granted, what its source was, and to what extent it was effective. But in less than two weeks, these *propositiones* had spread all through Germany, and in four weeks they were all over Christendom. It was as if the angels themselves worked as messengers to bring them before the eyes of all. No one can imagine how they were discussed. Soon they were translated into German and were welcomed by all, excepting the Dominicans and the bishop of Halle, and others who enjoyed the pope's favor and were becoming rich out of the funds he was raising.[38]

According to Luther's own testimony found in his writings in the years 1518–45, he approached the two bishops immediately concerned, Archbishop Albrecht of Magdeburg and Mainz, and Bishop Hieronymus Schulz of Brandenburg, the diocese in which Wittenberg lay. Luther begged them to take measures against the abuses arising from the preaching of indulgences. In the fifth and seventh citations, Luther speaks only of the bishop of Brandenburg, although in the fifth the phrasing, "I also warned him," indicates another addressee, probably Archbishop Albrecht. In the letter to Pope Leo X (our first citation) Luther speaks of privately warning a number of prelates ("*monui privatim aliquod Magnates Ecclesiarum*") and then tells of a threefold reaction. Therefore, others were involved beside Albrecht and Hieronymus, a fact which My-

[38] Myconius, *Geschichte der Reformation*, O. Clemen, ed. (Leipzig: n.d.), pp. 21f.

conius confirms by speaking of four bishops other than Albrecht.

Thus, there was a group of letters from Luther to different bishops. Unfortunately, none is extant except the letter of October 31, 1517, to Archbishop Albrecht. This letter's content leaves no doubt that it is one in the series here described. Before this time, Luther had not written to Archbishop Albrecht. In a letter to him on December 1, 1521, Luther noted that he had previously written Albrecht two Latin letters, "The first time was at the beginning of that mendacious indulgence which was issued under your electoral Grace's name. In that letter I faithfully warned your electoral Grace and opposed in Christian love the wild, seductive, and greedy preachers, and the heretical, superstitious books."[39]

Luther asserts that he wrote to different bishops, and specifically wrote to Archbishop Albrecht on October 31, 1517, at a time when none of his closest friends knew that he planned a disputation and before he issued his theses. It was only when the archbishop did not answer, and when the other bishops gave indecisive and evasive answers, that Luther issued his sheet of theses and invited scholars to dispute them with him. This, however, rules out a posting of the theses on the door of the castle church on October 31, 1517. For if Luther did post his theses then, he gave the bishops no time to react as he repeatedly claims to have done. If Luther posted his theses on All Saints' Eve then in the course of the year 1518 he deceived both the pope and Prince-elector Frederick, his own sovereign. For so soon after the event a slip of the memory was impossible. Finally, if Luther posted his theses on October 31, 1517, then he maintained a falsified version of these events even at the end of his life, when he had no need for diplomatically underplaying his own role by stressing the inertia of the bishops.

[39] WBr 2, 406, 3–8. LW 48, 339 (G. G. Krodel). Luther's second Latin letter is that of February 4, 1520 (WBr 2, 27–9). See Volz, *Martin Luthers Thesenanschlag*, p. 24; and his article "Erzbischof Albrecht von Mainz und Martin Luthers 95 Thesen," *Jahrbuch der Hessischen kirchengeschichtlichen Vereinigung*, XIII (1962), pp. 224f.

Some Luther scholars take into account what appears to be a lack of veracity on Luther's part, although most of them simply ignore this problem. Karl A. Meissinger wrote that Luther "put the events in order" for the benefit of Cardinal Cajetan, who was eventually to receive the matter given in Luther's letter to Frederick (our second citation). The same holds, according to Meissinger, for the letter to the pope (our first citation).[40] Kurt Aland explained that in this letter to Frederick in November, 1518, Luther spoke "tactically" and "with an eye toward the window," i.e., seeing the civil and ecclesiastical authorities.[41] Hans Volz found in this same letter, "a correction on diplomatic grounds for self-defense and self-justification."[42]

These explanations, however, are not convincing. It is in the letter to Frederick that Luther spoke of the earlier letter to Albrecht being extant (in copies) and having passed through many hands. Further, the posting of the theses by Luther is usually assumed to have been a widely known event. In these circumstances it would have been a quite clumsy tactic to juggle known and verifiable events in a letter written with an eye to a wider public. The same argument holds for Luther's preface to his Latin works in 1545 (our fourth citation). Perhaps he did not want to publicly take back the deceptive version he had given earlier.[43] But it was surely not prudent to repeat this story without cause, and this in the very volume containing the documents (theses, letter to Albrecht, etc.) by which one could check this account of the events.

Other researchers try to solve this dilemma and save Luther by explaining that even when printed theses were posted on the door of the castle church, still this would not

[40] *Der katholische Luther*, pp. 160, 167.

[41] *Martin Luthers 95 Thesen*, p. 120.

[42] Volz, *Theologische Literaturzeitung*, LXXXIX (1964), p. 682. Similarly G. Müller, "Die Diskussion über Luthers Thesenanschlag," *Pastoralblatt des evangelischen Pfarrervereins Kurhessen-Waldeck*, LXIV (1962), p. 117.

[43] Volz explained that the 1545 preface was so written as to agree with the May 1518 letter to Leo X and the November 1518 letter to Prince-elector Frederick. *Geschichte in Wissenschaft und Unterricht*, XVI (1965), p. 685, n. 8.

properly be a publication.[44] Even if this were correct, it would not remove the difficulty, for Luther did not only deny a publication of the theses, but he asserted that even his closest friends did not know that he was planning a disputation. (See WBr, 1, 245)

But what right do we have to charge Luther with this "tactical" lack of veracity? Or to put it another way: what makes us assume that Luther posted his theses on October 31, 1517, and thus left the bishops no time to react to his letters? What historical evidence is there of a posting of the theses on October 31, 1517?

[44] B. Lohse, "Der Stand der Debatte über Luthers Thesenanschlag," *Luther*, XXXIV (1963), p. 135. Aland (in "Luthers Thesenanschlag, Tatsache oder Legende?" *Deutsches Pfarrerblatt*, LXII [1962], p. 242) denies that a posting was a public circulation of the theses. But on the next page he argues that Luther's words about having invited publicly to a disputation, "*publice, ante fores*," are proof that he did post the theses on the church door.

V. LUTHER AND HIS CONTEMPORARIES ON THE OUTBREAK OF THE INDULGENCE CONTROVERSY

WE MUST FIRST ASK whether there is any contemporary testimony witnessing to Luther's posting of his theses. There appears to be no dearth of reports about Luther's entry onto the public scene and about the indulgence controversy. As authority for the posting of the theses on October 31, 1517, writers on Luther have up to now ordinarily assumed Luther's servant, Johannes Agricola (born Schneider), to have been an eyewitness. The otherwise quite reliable book of Heinrich Boehmer, *Martin Luther: Road to Reformation*, gives this account:

> . . . he [Luther] said nothing of his project to any of his friends and colleagues; nor did he show anyone the placard containing the ninety-five theses on the power and efficacy of indulgences. Thus no one in Wittenberg suspected what he had in mind until, on the eve of All Saints (October 31) 1517, shortly before twelve o'clock noon, accompanied only by his famulus, Johannes Schneider of Eisleben, called Agricola, he walked from the Black Cloister to the castle church, about fifteen minutes away, and there on the door of the north entrance, which had often been used as a bulletin board before the great festivals, he nailed the placard with the ninety-five theses.[1]

[1] Heinrich Boehmer, *Martin Luther, Road to Reformation*, translated by John W. Doberstein and Theodore G. Tappert (London: Meridian, 1957), p. 184. A similar interpretation is given in these works: *Realencyklopädie für protestantische Theologie und Kirche*, I, 250; G. Kawerau, *Johannes Agricola* (Berlin: 1881), p. 16; Meissinger, *Der katholische Luther* (Munich: 1952), p. 130; *Neue deutsche Biographie*, I, 100; Aland, "Der 31. 10. 1517 gilt zu Recht als Tag des Thesenanschlages Martin Luthers," *Deutsches Pfarrerblatt*, LVIII (1958), pp. 241–5.

However, Boehmer's description is based on a mistaken translation of an autobiographical note attributed to Agricola. There the supposed text reads, "Anno 1517 proposuit Lutherus Witenbergae, quae urbs est ad Albim sita, pro veteri scholarum more themata quaedam disputanda, me teste quidem citra ullius hominis aut notam aut iniuriam."[2] In translation: "In the year 1517 Luther presented in Wittenberg on the Elbe some theses for disputation according to the custom of scholars. His purpose, as I can testify, was in no way to insult or injure anyone." This source gives no date, nor does it mention a posting on the door of the castle church. And the "*me teste*" does not mean "as I witnessed," referring to the event itself, as Boehmer inferred, but refers to Luther's intention and motivation. Furthermore, "*me teste*" was not just misunderstood, the phrase was itself the product of a false reading. As Hans Volz has reported, the "*me teste*" stems from a misreading of Agricola's jottings, where the reading "*modeste*" (i.e., "modestly," modifying *proposuit*) is clearly to be preferred.[3] This removes the last ground for considering Agricola as an eye witness of a theses posting.

From Luther himself, besides the statements we gave in the previous chapter which add up to a clear case against a posting of the theses on October 31, 1517, there are two other pieces of evidence to be considered.

1. In 1527 Luther wrote to Nicolas Amsdorf, a former canon of the All Saints' Church in Wittenberg, and dated his letter thus: "Wittenberg, All Saints' Day, 1527, ten years after indulgences were destroyed. Let us both drink to their memory —consoled in this hour."[4]

Here Luther indicates that he struck the decisive blow

[2] A. Brecher, "Neue Beiträge zum Briefwechsel der Reformatoren," *Zeitschrift für historische Theologie*, XLII (1872), p. 326. See also Volz, *Martin Luthers Thesenanschlag und dessen Vorgeschichte*, p. 103, n. 150.

[3] W. E. Peuckert, "Agricola," *Handwörterbuch der Sage*, I (Göttingen: 1961), col. 171, n. 5, and Volz, "Erzbischof Albrecht von Mainz und Martin Luthers 95 Thesen," *Jahrbuch der Hessischen kirchengeschichtlichen Vereinigung*, XIII (1962), p. 227, n. 159.

[4] In the original: "Wittembergae die Omnium Sanctorum anno decimo Indulgentiarum conculcatarum, quarum memoria hac hora bibimus utrinque consolati, 1527." WBr 4, 275, 25ff.

against indulgences on All Saints' Day, which can just as well mean the afternoon of October 31 as November 1 itself. However, we do full justice to this evidence by supposing that Luther sent his theses to the competent church authorities on October 31.

2. Between January and March, 1532, Luther made a remark at table that agrees with what we have seen: "In the year 1517 I began on the feast of All Saints to write against the pope and against indulgences."[5]

Luther spoke on other occasions about writing against the pope or against indulgences[6] and about issuing or submitting his theses,[7] but never did he mention a posting of the theses on the door of the castle church. The phrasing "began . . . to write" in the last citation does not allow us to conclude that a unique event like a posting of the theses occurred, but rather places the events of October 31, 1517, in a series with Luther's later writings.

Among the numerous other sources that up to the time of Luther's death speak of the indulgence theses and Luther's action against Tetzel's preaching and Albrecht's *instructio* there is not one word about a posting of the theses, to say nothing about such an event on October 31, or November 1, 1517. Among Protestant contemporaries of Luther who do not mention the event are the chroniclers, Christoph Scheurl,[8]

[5] "Anno 17. in die omnium sanctorum incepi primum scribere contra papam et indulgentias." WTr 2, 467, n. 2455a. The alternate version, n. 2455b, gives "*in festo*," as we translated above, instead of "*in die*." But in both cases the afternoon of October 31 is included, a fact which the bull granting indulgence privileges to the Church of All Saints confirms: "Item ipso die omnium sanctorum vere confessi et contriti aut bonam intentionem habentes a primis vesperis usque ad secundas inclusive possunt mereri ipsas indulgentias suis orationibus et elemosinis." Given by J. Haussleiter, *Die Universität Wittenberg vor dem Eintritt Luthers* (Leipzig: 1903), p. 26. Accordingly, the day of All Saints begins with first vespers in the afternoon of the vigil. This would remove the cogency from Volz' argument from this table remark and from the letter to Amsdorf for a theses posting on November 1, instead of on October 31.

[6] WTr 1, 441, n. 884; WTr 2, 376, n. 2250; WTr 3, 477, n. 3644c.

[7] See the texts given above, pp. 56–60.

[8] "Ursprung und Anfang Lutherischer Handlung" in *Geschichtsbuch der Christenheit von 1511 bis 1521*, edited by J. K. F. Knaake in *Jahrbücher des deutschen Reiches und deutschen Kirche im Zeitalter der Reformation*, I (Leipzig: 1872), pp. 111ff.

Johann Carion,[9] Friedrich Myconius,[10] Georg Spalatin,[11] and Johannes Sleidanus.[12] Neither do the Catholics Kilian Leib,[13] Johannes Cochläus,[14] or Hieronymus Emser[15] know of a posting of the theses.

We can omit a detailed treatment of all of these texts, but at least the chronicle of Johann Carion (1499–1537/38) merits special attention. Carion was a mathematician and astrologer at the court of the prince-elector, Joachim I of Brandenburg, and his work went through many editions in German, Latin, and in other languages. However, both as to method and content, the actual author was Philipp Melanchthon.[16] In 1531

[9] See on Carion: *Neue deutsche Biographie* (Berlin: 1953—), III, 138; and Volz, *Martin Luthers Thesenanschlag*, p. 93, n. 107, which refers to *Beiträge zur Geschichte der deutschen Sprache und Literatur*, LXXVII (Tübingen: 1955), p. 415, n. 3, where literature on Carion is listed.

[10] See above, pp. 60–61.

[11] Spalatin, who was a close friend of Luther in 1517, makes no mention of a posting of theses in the chronicles he wrote. See Volz, *Martin Luthers Thesenanschlag*, p. 93, n. 110.

[12] In the *Commentarii*, a chronicle begun before 1545 and published in 1555, there is no mention of Luther's posting of the theses. In Book I for 1517 we read the following after mention of Luther's letter to Archbishop Albrecht on indulgences: "Cum iis literis una mittebat themata, quae nuper disputandi causa Wittenbergae promulgabat."

[13] "Id cum persensisset Martinus Luther qui tunc Wittenbergae agebat, Problemata scribere coepit, quae vocant Propositiones de Indulgentiis, de earum valore deque romani pontificis potestate, quae omnia in dubium: nescio an ducis Friderici principis iussu, an impulsu daemonis hospitis sui, an suopte ingenio." From Leib's *Annales*, edited by J. C. von Aretin in *Beiträge zur Geschichte und Literatur*, VII (Munich: 1806), pp. 665f. See also J. Deutsch, *Kilian Leib* (Münster: 1910), pp. 162f. In his diary Leib made this brief entry for 1518: "Hoc tempore Martini Lutheri haeretici Wittenbergii propositiones theologicae sermonesque seu sermo alter quidam Latine, alius vulgato editio eloquio circumferebantur, quibus praesertim de indulgentiis, quas pontifices elargiri solent, disserebatur." J. Schlecht, *Kilian Leibs Briefwechsel und Diarien* (Münster: 1906), p. 85.

[14] Cochläus speaks in his *Commentaria* of the letter to Albrecht on October 31, 1517, and then continues, "Ille tamen non contentus privatam misisse epistolam, in publicum quoque emulgavit 95 (quamquam in prima scheda posuerit 97) propositiones." Cited by Volz, *Martin Luthers Thesenanschlag*, p. 93, n. 108. See also A. Herte, *Die Lutherkommentare des Johannes Cochläus* (Münster: 1935), p. 276.

[15] Emser wrote in his 1521 reply "to the Ox of Wittenberg," that first of all Luther had heretical theses printed against Tetzel, thus defying all theologians, and that he wanted to defend the theses before them. L. Enders, *Luther und Emser* (Halle: 1891), II, 31.

[16] R. Stupperich, *Der unbekannte Melanchthon* (Stuttgart: 1961), p. 78.

Carion handed over to Melanchthon for reworking the material he had gathered. Melanchthon brought the work out in German in 1532 under a title that credited Carion's work in collecting the material.[17] In 1537 a Latin translation appeared.[18] In all the editions appearing before 1546, there is no report of Luther posting his theses. We simply read, "In 1517, when Leo was pope, Martin Luther wrote for the first time against indulgences. This gave rise to many disputations, and as a result there has been a great schism in Germany."[19]

There is a second text which we cannot omit, since it is frequently brought forth as a proof that Luther's theses were posted on the door of the castle church. This interpretation is only possible, however, when one comes upon the text with a preconceived opinion. In a table remark Friedrich Myconius told of Luther's grave illness while in Schmalkald and in

[17] "Chronica durch Magistrum Johann Carion vleissig zusamen gezogen meniglich nützlich zu lesen, Gedruckt zu Wittenberg durch Georgen Rhaw." Carion's dedication of the work is from 1531, but at the end of the chronicle the year 1532 is mentioned (CLXVIII–CLXIX). See G. T. Strobel (editor), *Miscellaneen Literarischen Inhalts grösstentheils aus ungedruckten Quellen . . . Sechste Sammlung* (Nürnberg: 1782), p. 163.

[18] "Chronica Joannis Carionis conversa ex Germanica in Latinum a doctissimo viro Hermanno Bono, et ab autore diligenter recognita. Halae Sueuorum ex officina Petri Brubachii, 1537." Strobel, *Miscellaneen*, p. 173.

[19] "Zur zeit Leonis anno 1517 hat Martinus Luther erstlich widder den Ablas geschrieben, und sind hernach viel disputationes erreget. Daraus nu ein grosse spaltung inn Deudschland worden ist." Wittenberg edition (see n. 17 above), fol. 166v, ll. 21–4. See Strobel, *Miscellaneen*, p. 164. A Magdeburg German edition from the press of Christian Roediger (without date) gives the same information as the Wittenberg edition of 1532, fol. Aa iiij^{v}, ll. 22–7. Also this is repeated in a Latin edition printed by Peter Brubach in Frankfurt in 1543, fol. 237v, ll. 21ff. But the Wittenberg Latin edition of 1572 has been revised, obviously to agree with Melanchthon's preface to the second volume of Luther's works, and tells of the theses being posted on the door of the castle church on October 31, 1517: "Eo igitur anno, qui fuit septimus decimus supra millesimum, quingentesimum, Lutherus primum oppugnare coepit forum indulgenitiarum, et ex ecclesia filii Dei, huius ipsius Domini nostri Jesu Christi exemplo eijcere ementes et vendentes, eversis mensis scabellisque; . . . Disputatio proposita est in foribus templi, quod arci Witebergensi contiguum est, pridie Calend. Novembris tali occasione et initio: Circumferebantur titulo Alverti Archiepiscopi Magdeburgensis venales indulgentiae in his regionibus a Tecelio Dominicano Sycophanta impudentissimo. Huius impiis et nefariis concionibus irritatus Lutherus, studio pietatis ardens, edidit (265^{r}:) propositiones de indulgentiis, quae in primo Tomo monumentorum ipsius extant. . . . Propositiones etiam et concionem de indulgentiis Lutheri conijcit in flammas . . ."

Gotha in 1537. Luther felt he was near death and spoke of dying and being buried in Gotha. Myconius had sought to calm him by saying that the illness was not so serious as Luther thought. However, if Luther were to die, Myconius promised to see to it that he would be buried in the church in Wittenberg, from which source the word of God had flowed over the whole world.[20]

Hans Volz saw in this text an obvious reference by Myconius to the castle church in Wittenberg and to the posting of the theses.[21] However, the text makes no mention of the castle church nor of a posting of the theses. Myconius could just as well have meant the parish church of Wittenberg, in which Luther had preached the word of God for more than twenty years. Volz simply assumes that in 1537 the castle church was already decided upon as the place where Luther would be buried. Against such a supposition we have the letter of March 7, 1546, in which Adam Lindemann, then a student in Wittenberg, tells that after Luther's death there was some discussion about the place of his burial.[22]

Even if Myconius were speaking of the castle church, why must that involve a reference to a posting of the theses? In

[20] "*. . . vellem curare ut Vitebergae in ecclesia, in qua fons vitae profluxisset in orbem terrae, sepeliretur.*" WTr 3, 394, n. 3543. An improved reading of this remark has been made: "*si moreretur, velle se curare, ut Wittenbergae in ecclesia, ex qua fons verbi divini profluxisset in orbem terrarum, sepeliretur.*" *Archiv für Reformationgeschichte*, XXI (1934), p. 259.

[21] *Martin Luthers Thesenanschlag und dessen Vorgeschichte*, p. 94, n. 115. Another participant in the discussion (K. Harms, "Noch einmal: Luthers Thesenanschlag," *Deutsches Pfarrerblatt*, LXIII [1963], p. 520) cited Luther's remark to Myconius as irrefutable proof that the theses were posted on the door of the castle church. Harms, however, failed even to mention the arguments I had put forth in my lecture and booklet of 1962 that show this text to be quite irrelevant for proving a posting of the theses. Also H. Steubing ("Hat Luther die 95 Thesen wirklich angeschlagen?" *Kirche in der Zeit*, XX [1965], p. 452) failed to tell his readers of my arguments (in a review of my book) and then went on to find this remark to Myconius confirming the posting of the theses. On Steubing's method of argumentation, see above, p. 55, n. 24.

[22] "De sepulcri loco est deliberatum: sed Illustrissimo Principi nostro fuit obsequendum mandanti, ut in templo arcis Vitenbergensis iuxta monumenta suorum maiorum Ducum illustrissimorum sepeliretur." Given in *Die Berichte über Luthers Tod und Begräbnis*, edited by Christoph Schubert (Weimar: 1917), p. 53.

Detail from "*L'affichage des thèses par Luther*"
in the Bibliothèque Nationale, Paris

the many reports about Luther's burial there is no mention of him having posted his theses, to say nothing of that as the precise motive for his burial in the castle church. Near the princes' vault was the pulpit from which Luther had preached the word of God, and that was mentioned as a factor in choosing the location of the grave.[23] The latter fits well with Myconius' words "*fons verbi divini.*"

We hardly need to note that there is no pictorial evidence from before Luther's death that would support a theses posting. An apparent problem is the quite theatrical presentation in the engraving "*L'affichage des thèses par Luther*" in the Cabinet des Estampes of the Bibliothèque Nationale in Paris. This had been dated in 1527 by É. G. Léonard.[24] However, the Bibliothèque Nationale has informed me that there is no known evidence in support of this dating. In fact the engraving itself offers many reasons which exclude such an early dating. Omitting discussion of the style, which suggests a considerably later dating, two facts are immediately apparent: 1. The inscription in the lower right corner dedicates the engraving to "Friedrich Christoph, Graf and Lord of Mansfeld." But only two possibilities are to be found among the Mansfeld nobility: a Friedrich Christoph, who lived 1564–1631, and a Christoph, who ruled 1558–91.[25] 2. The scripture texts given to explain the various scenes on the engraving follow exactly the 1545 edition of Luther's translation of the Bible.

Thus, neither Luther himself nor the numerous witnesses speak during Luther's lifetime of a posting of the indulgence theses on the door of the castle church in Wittenberg. Who then first reported such an event?

[23] For example in the reports of Justus Jonas, Michael Cölius, and J. Aurifaber on Luther's burial. *Ibid.*, p. 68.

[24] *Histoire générale du Protestantisme, La Réformation* (Paris: 1961), I, 80–1. These pages give a reproduction of the engraving. To the title the year "1527" is added.

[25] See Frank Baron Freytag von Loringhoven, *Europäische Stammtafeln* (Marburg: 1956), III, tab. 44.

The source was no less a personage than Philipp Melanchthon, in the preface to the second volume of Luther's collected works, published after Luther's death. There we read, "Luther, burning with zeal for true piety, issued indulgence theses which are printed in the first volume of this series. He posted these theses publicly at the church near the castle in Wittenberg on the vigil of All Saints' Day in 1517."[26] This sentence from Melanchthon is obviously the basis for the later reports about a posting of the theses.

There can be no doubt that the testimony of a man so close to Luther and so important for the Reformation in Wittenberg as Melanchthon carries considerable weight.

One point is clear from the start: in 1517 Melanchthon was still in Tübingen and therefore could have known of the events of this year in Wittenberg only from verbal report. Furthermore, before 1546, Melanchthon makes no mention of the theses being posted. For instance, in February 1521, he wrote under the pseudonym Didymus Faventius in Luther's defense against the Roman Dominican Tommaso Rhadino. In this work he relates that Luther, in fulfilling his duty as pastor, very modestly presented some paradoxical sentences on indulgences. These were not definitive assertions but only theses for a customary disputation. Further, Luther warned the people in a sermon against paying too much for these Roman wares. Shortly afterwards, he gave more extensive arguments for his theses in the book of resolutions.[27]

In later letters written by Melanchthon on October 31,

[26] "In hoc cursu cum esset Lutherus, circumferuntur venales indulgentiae in his regionibus a Tecelio Dominicano impudentissimo sycophanta, cuius impiis et nefariis concionibus irritatus Lutherus, studio pietatis ardens, edidit Propositiones de Indulgentiis, quae in primo Tomo monumentorum ipsius extant, Et has publice Templo, quod arci Witebergensi contiguum est, affixit pridie festi omnium Sanctorum anno 1517." *Corpus Reformatorum*, VI, cols. 161f.

[27] "Facturus boni pastoris officium, proposuit quaedam de Indulgentiis paradoxa, idque modeste, nihil statuens aut decernens, sed disputans tantum pro more scholarum." *Ibid.*, I, col. 291. In a letter to Oekolampadius, July 21, 1519, Melanchthon spoke of Eck's critical remarks about the "*sententias, quas Martinus de indulgentia proposuit disputandas.*" *Ibid.*, cols. 88f.

the first reference to the indulgence theses comes in 1552.[28] After this he speaks frequently (though not always)[29] on this annual date about the theses being issued (*edidit*) or presented (*proposuit*).[30]

Melanchthon had no direct knowledge of events in Wittenberg before 1518, and in speaking about them he shows himself in many respects poorly informed. In a first draft of the preface of the Augsburg Confession written in May 1530, he states, for example, that the St. Peter's indulgence was preached in Saxony.[31] However, we know that both of the Saxon rulers, Prince-elector Frederick the Wise and Duke George, refused Tetzel permission to preach in their territories.[32] In the preface to the second volume of Luther's works, Melanchthon propagated the legend that Tetzel had publicly burned Luther's theses and a sermon on indul-

[28] Earlier letters written on October 31 are extant from 1524 (*Corpus Reformatorum*, I, 678–81, 682–3), 1526 (*Ibid.*, 827ff.), 1531 (*Ibid.*, II, 549f.), and 1537 (*Ibid.*, III, 439f.) None of these letters refers to the publication of the theses. But at the end of a letter to Sebastian Glaser, October 31, 1552, Melanchthon wrote, "*Pridie Calend. Novemb. quo primum ante annos 35 Lutherus Propositiones de indulgentiis* . . . ," *Ibid.*, VII, 1122.

[29] Volz wrote that Melanchthon always mentioned the posting of the theses in letters on October 31 in the years after 1552. *Martin Luthers Thesenanschlag und dessen Vorgeschichte*, p. 36. This is not true, however, since there is no mention of it in the letter of this date in 1553 (*Corpus Reformatorum*, VIII, 167f.) nor in the three letters on this day in 1557 (*Ibid.*, IX, 357f.).

[30] For example, in letters of October 31, 1555 (*Ibid.*, VIII, 594f.), and 1559 (*Ibid.*, IX, 956). Also in his postil from 1557, Melanchthon spoke of the posting of the theses: "Ultimus autem dies Oktobris . . . est dies ille, quo primum propositae sunt propositiones D. Lutheri de indulgentiis, quae fuerunt initium emendationis doctrinae . . . Fuerunt affixae templo Arcis ad vespertinam concionem. . . . Mementote ergo hunc diem." *Ibid.*, XXV, col. 777. See Volz, *Martin Luthers Thesenanschlag und dessen Vorgeschichte*, p. 95, n. 118. Carion's chronicle, which was issued by Melanchthon, mentions the posting of the theses only in the years after 1546.

[31] *Bekenntnisschriften der evangelisch-lutherischen Kirche* (4th ed.; Göttingen: 1959), p. 41. In 1521 Melanchthon could write, "Et ut inde ordiamur, unde omnis haec tragoedia orta est, anno abhinc tertio Romanenses indulgentiae quas vocant, in Saxonas ac Mysos, nescio quorum praepostera liberalitate, profundebantur." In "Didymi Faventini . . . oratio," *Corpus Reformatorum*, I, col. 291.

[32] Schulte, *Die Fugger in Rom*, I, 142f. Volz, *Martin Luthers Thesenanschlag und dessen Vorgeschichte*, p. 101, n. 141.

gences. Further Melanchthon falsely dated Luther's trip to Rome as 1511, had Luther lecturing in Wittenberg on physics instead of ethics,[33] and placed Luther's lectures on the Psalms (actually 1513–15) after the lectures on Romans (1515–16). These and other errors were the grounds for this adverse judgment on Melanchthon by Heinrich Boehmer: "The famous preface is nothing more than a preface, that is, a piece dashed off quickly without use of any sources. Thus it has no value as documentation and is to be believed only to the extent that contemporary witnesses offer confirmation."[34]

Even Hans Volz felt compelled to judge Melanchthon's narrative as "an untenable legend."[35] Why then should we not say the same about Melanchthon's report on Luther posting his theses? No one else reports it, and Luther spoke clearly and frequently in a manner that excludes such a posting.[36]

[33] Although WTr 1, 44, n. 116, has it that Luther did teach physics.

[34] H. Boehmer, *Luthers Romfahrt (1510–11)* (Leipzig: 1914), p. 8.

[35] *Martin Luthers Thesenanschlag und dessen Vorgeschichte*, p. 37. Aland would still view Melanchthon's preface as reliable, especially in view of the greater inaccuracies of people like Luther's own son. "Der Thesenanschlag fand—und zwar am 31. Oktober—statt," *Geschichte in Wissenschaft und Unterricht*, XVI (November, 1965), p. 693.

[36] Honselmann rightly questions why Volz' judgment against Melanchthon's preface as an historical source does not also cast doubt on the event of the theses posting, especially since Volz has seen that Luther himself never mentioned the posting. *Urfassung und Drucke der Ablassthesen Martin Luthers* (Paderborn: 1966), p. 26, n. 31.

VI. THE THESES WERE NOT POSTED!

THE MAIN ARGUMENT against a public posting of the ninety-five theses is Luther's own statement that he issued his theses only after receiving no answer to his letter of October 31, 1517, to the archbishop of Magdeburg and Mainz. In addition there is a series of further facts that argue against such a posting.

1. On February 2, 1538, Luther related the following at table:

> God has led us along in a wonderful way and has guided me even without my knowing it for more than twenty years. How troublesome it was at the beginning, as we went to Kemberg, after All Saints' in 1517. It was then that I undertook to write against the blatant errors on indulgences. But Dr. Hieronymus Schurff tried to stop me, "What! You want to attack the pope? That they will not allow!" But I said, "And if they must allow it?"[1]

Thus, sometime after All Saints' Day, 1517, Luther walked to Kemberg, eight miles south of Wittenberg, and on the way startled his friend, Professor Hieronymus Schurff, with the revelation that he planned to write against indulgences. Schurff was Luther's colleague and was well informed about university affairs in Wittenberg. But Luther could still surprise Schurff with his plan, even after All Saints' Day. This rules out a posting of the theses before or on the feast of All Saints',

[1] WTr 3, 564, n. 3722.

and it further confirms Luther's assertion that when he wrote to the bishops even his closest friends did not know of his intention of holding a disputation.

2. The same holds for Luther's friend and fellow Augustinian, Johannes Lang, the prior of the order's house in Erfurt. On the occasion of his earlier disputation against scholastic theology, September 4, 1517, Luther had sent Lang a copy of the theses even before the disputation was held. Luther himself judged these earlier theses to be of greater importance than his indulgence theses, since in fact they attacked both the theology and the church of the late Middle Ages more sharply and more centrally than did the ninety-five indulgence theses. On the day of the disputation in Wittenberg Luther wrote to Lang and offered to dispute the theses publicly in Erfurt as well, either in the university or in the Augustinian priory. People should not think that he "wants to whisper these matters in a corner, if it be that the Wittenberg university is so insignificant to be thought of as being only a corner."[2]

This letter shows Luther in lively theological exchange with Lang. Further, it shows that Wittenberg ranked as a far corner of the theological world, a city therefore which did not offer Luther the wider theological public he sought.

Luther waited until November 11, 1517, to send his ninety-five indulgence theses to Lang. He wanted to hear what Lang and the other Erfurt Augustinians thought of them, and especially he wanted to have errors in them pointed out if any could be found. But Luther, who had earlier defended himself against the charge of being an arrogant critic, did not want people to misunderstand the significance of his sending theses to Erfurt. This was not an act of humility, as if he felt he needed their advice and decision before publishing his

[2] ". . . me scilicet esse paratissimum venire et publice seu in collegio seu in monasterio de iis disputare, ut non putent me in angulum ista velle susurrare, si tamen nostra universitas tam vilis est, ut angulus esse possit videri." WBr 1, 103, 12–5.

theses.[3] This last remark makes it necessary to suppose that the theses were not as yet published on November 11, 1517.

Klemens Honselmann has questioned whether the theses which were called "*paradoxa*" in the covering letter sent to Lang on November 11 were the indulgence theses.[4] Honselmann contends that Luther spoke of the latter as "*positiones*," "*propositiones*," "*conclusiones*," and "*disputationes*," but never as "*paradoxa*." Luther, however, commonly referred to theses as "*paradoxa*," and did not reserve the term to theses on philosophical subjects. For example, in a letter to Scheurl on May 6, 1517, he called Carlstadt's 151 theses on the theology of Augustine "*positiones*" and "*paradoxa*" (WBr 1, 94, 15ff.) In 1521 Melanchthon called Luther's indulgence theses "*paradoxa*."[5] Therefore, the term cannot be used to prove that the theses sent to Lang on November 11, 1517, were philosophical theses.

Honselmann argued further that the content of this letter to Lang on November 11 could not possibly accompany a covering letter for theses on indulgences, because the letter speaks about Aristotle and the scholastics. But this is not convincing when one examines the context in which Aristotle is mentioned. After presenting his theses in September against scholastic theology, Luther was charged with intellectual arrogance. Now, as he sends another list of theses, he defends himself in advance against charges of frivolous and presumptuous criticism. This he does by pointing out how Aristotle was a faultfinder in almost every line he wrote. The scholastics were nothing but critics who were constantly finding fault with each other's positions. Thus, Luther's reference to

[3] "Ecce alia denuo Paradoxa mitto, Reverendissime Pater mi in Christo." WBr 1, 121, 4. ". . . Id solum cupio ex te tuisque theologis quam maximo voto, tacito interim autoris vitio, de ipsis editionibus meis vel conclusionibus quid sentiant, intelligere, imo multo magis erroris vitia, si qua in illis sunt, mihi significari. . . . Non itaque volo, eam ex me expectent humilitatem (id est hypocrisin), ut prius eorum consilio et decreto mihi utendum esse credant, quam edam." WBr 1, 122, 35ff.

[4] Honselmann, *Urfassung und Drucke der Ablassthesen Martin Luthers*, pp. 106f.

[5] *Corpus Reformatorum*, I, col. 291. See p. 73, n. 27, above.

Aristotle and the scholastics did not pertain to philosophical content in his theses, but to the critical method. He wants to show that criticism is not the same as arrogance. Since Luther's indulgence theses were no less critical in tone than the theses against scholastic theology, he knows that the charge of arrogance might well be raised against him in Erfurt. Luther therefore seeks to defend himself against such a superficial and prejudiced charge which pays no attention to the matter under discussion. Since we know of no other theses of Luther's at this time, we can assume that the theses sent to Lang on November 11 were the ninety-five indulgence theses.

Luther thus waited almost two weeks before sending the theses to his close friends in the Erfurt priory. Therefore, at this time he still supposed that they would be unknown there. Later in *Wider Hans Worst* (1541), Luther asserted that the theses spread all through Germany in fourteen days. (W 51, 540, 26)

Luther did still allow a period to pass within which he could have received an answer from the bishops. For Halle, where Luther thought Albrecht was staying at Moritzburg, Albrecht's favorite residence, is only forty-five miles from Wittenberg. Brandenburg, the home of Luther's ordinary, Bishop Hieronymus, was only fifty miles away. Even considering sixteenth-century postal methods, Luther could reasonably have expected some answer by November 11.[6] The fact that Luther's letter of October 31 was opened and copied by Albrecht's councillors in Calbe on the Saale only on November 17 was surely due to causes other than the postal methods.

3. Luther repeatedly said that he distributed his theses to scholars, both in Wittenberg and in other cities.[7] Johannes

[6] Thus I do not agree with G. Müller, *Pastoralblatt des evangelischen Pfarrvereins Kurhessen-Waldeck*, LXIV (1962), p. 197.

[7] "Itaque schedulam disputatoriam edidi invitans tantum doctiores." Letter to Pope Leo X, May 1518; W 1, 528, 24f. ". . . non fuit consilium neque votum eas evulgari, sed cum paucis apud et circum nos habitantibus primum super ipsis conferri, ut sic multorum iudicio vel damnatae abolerentur vel probatae ederentur." Letter to Scheurl, March 5, 1518; WBr 1, 152, 7ff. See also

Lang would be one of these scholars, as we saw above. The title placed over the theses also points to such a procedure, but it seems to be a serious mistake to use this title as a proof that Luther posted the theses. This will be clear if we only compare this title with the title of the theses for the disputation held in Wittenberg in 1516 on the powers and the will of man without grace. This earlier title reads:

> Under the illustrious man Martin Luther, Augustinian and Master of both Arts and Theology, the following question will be disputed next Friday at 7:00 A.M. (W 1, 145)

The title of the indulgence theses of 1517 reads:

> Out of love and zeal for truth and the desire to bring it to light, the following theses will be publicly discussed at Wittenberg under the chairmanship of the Reverend Father Martin Luther, Master of Arts and Sacred Theology and regularly appointed lecturer on these subjects at that place. He requests that those who cannot be present to debate orally with us will do so by letter.[8]

The point is that the request for written contributions does not make sense if the theses were posted on the university bulletin board to announce a disputation within the univer-

---

Luther's letter to J. Trutfetter on May 9, 1518, WBr 1, 170. 41ff. In Luther's *Asterisci* against Eck, he wrote, "Nam cum ego non lingua vulgari aediderim nec latius quam circum nos emiserim, adde solum doctioribus obtulerim et amicis eruditioribus." W 1, 311, 19f.

[8] W 1, 233. LW 31, 25 (C. M. Jacobs and Harold J. Grimm). Honselmann pointed out (*Urfassung und Drucke*, p. 56f.) that the Roman theologian Silvester Prierias did not give this title with its announcement and request for written contributions in his *Dialogus* (June 1518), where he gives the text of Luther's theses. This follows with Honselmann's theory that Prierias, as master of the sacred palace, had before him the copy of the theses that Archibishop Albrecht had sent on to Rome. This would be a copy of the theses Luther had sent to the archbishop, and here this title would not have appeared. There was no point in scheduling a disputation so long as there was still a chance that Albrecht would recall his *instructio* and urge restraint on the indulgence preachers. But the title is not the only thing missing in Prierias' version of the theses. He does not give Theses 92 and 93. Honselmann sees these as Luther's later additions in response to the attack by Wimpina and Tetzel, see below, pp. 87–88.

sity. This title suggests rather a distribution of the theses by mail or perhaps circulation of printed copies.

4. But the fact is that no disputation was held. It was not that Luther did not want a disputation in Wittenberg but that he could find no opponent. If he as *Magister regens* had announced a disputation, then he also would have named the *opponens* and *respondens*, or had these named by the dean of the faculty.

But Luther was not thinking of a specific discussion partner in the narrower circles of Wittenberg. At least his repeated assertions lead us to suppose that he did not intend to hold one of the usual circular or graduation disputations.[9] On this point the researchers are in agreement.[10]

But if Luther was thinking of a disputation before a wider public, for example one such as was held in Leipzig in 1519, then a posting of the theses in Wittenberg was not a suitable

[9] "... respondeo, quod non fuit consilium neque votum eas evulgari, sed cum paucis apud et circum nos habitantibus primum super ipsis conferri, ut sic multorum iudicio vel damnatae abolerentur vel probatae ederentur." Letter to Scheurl, March 5, 1518, WBr 1, 152, 7–10. "... *apud nos et propter nostros tantum sunt editae* ..." Letter to Pope Leo X, W 1, 528, 38.

[10] E. Wolf judged it unlikely that Luther presented his theses for a circular disputation, nor for any other kind of disputation foreseen by the statutes of the university. The fact that no disputation took place indicates that Luther intended an extraordinary disputation similar to that in Liepzig in 1519. "Zur wissenschaftlichen Bedeutung der Disputation an der Wittenberger Universität im 16. Jahrhundert," in *450 Jahre Martin-Luther-Universität* (1952), I, 336. If the theses were meant for a circular disputation (held on Friday), then according to the statutes (see n. 13, below) they should have been posted on Thursday, and not on Saturday, October 31. Volz also concluded that Luther intended a disputation somewhat independent of the university as in Leipzig in 1519. "Der Thesenanschlag fand—und wahrscheinlich am 1. November 1517—statt," *Geschichte in Wissenschaft und Unterricht*, XVI (November 1965), pp. 684f. See also Honselmann, *Urfassung und Drucke*, pp. 24f. In the report written for Archbishop Albrecht by the university faculty in Mainz (see above, p. 55) the theses are however so described: "*conclusiones seu positiones ... in insigni universali gymnasio Wittenburgensi scolastice et publice disputatas*." *Zeitschrift für Kirchengeschichte*, XXIII (1902), pp. 266f. The Mainz professors would have falsely supposed that a disputation had taken place, reasoning from ordinary university practice. However, the copy of the theses they had received from the archbishop would not have had the title later printed above the theses indicating no set time and calling for written contributions.

way to make this known. The theses for such a disputation were mailed out or circulated in printed copies. If participants came forward, and if the place, time, and a more precise topic were fixed, then the theses would be posted at the place of the disputation. But all this did not happen with Luther's indulgence theses, since upon being circulated they found such a positive echo and such wide acceptance that the disputation became superfluous. In fact Luther's concern was that the theses which he had put up only for debate and without identifying himself with them were being taken as an expression of his own position.[11] For this reason he went on to write the more popular "Sermon on Indulgences and Grace" and the *Resolutiones* to explain his exact position. In both writings Luther sought to prevent erroneous interpretations being made of his ideas and intentions drawn from the theses alone.

Perhaps one reason why the disputation did not take place was that the theses had become a political factor. The rumor spread that the theses were inspired by Frederick the Wise as a blow at his rival, Albrecht of Magdeburg. On the other hand, Luther complained in letters that no one came forward to take part in a public discussion on indulgences.[12]

Moreover, the statutes of the university required that theses for university disputations would be made public by the dean by being posted on the doors of the churches—therefore not only the castle church—and within the university itself.[13] The posting was not done personally by the professor,

[11] "Inter quae sunt, quae dubito, Nonnulla ignoro, aliqua et nego, Nulla vero pertinaciter assero." To Bishop Hieronymus in Brandenburg, WBr 1, 139, 52. "Disputationes sunt, non doctrinae, non dogmata, obscurius pro more et enygmaticos positae." To Pope Leo, W 1, 528, 39ff. "Sunt enim nonnulla mihi ipsi dubia." To Scheurl, WBr 1, 152, 13.

[12] To Spalatin, February 15, 1518, WBr 1, 146, 86ff. To Bishop Hieronymus, February 13, 1518, WBr 1, 139, 46. See these texts below, p. 96 and p. 92, respectively.

[13] One of the duties of the dean of the theological faculty was this: "Promotiones similiter et disputationes intimet valuis ecclesiarum feria praecedente specivocando nomina promotoris, promovendi, praesidentis et respondentis . . ." *Die Wittenberger Universitäts- und Fakultätsstatuten vom Jahre 1508*, edited by T. Muther (Halle: 1867), p. 18. Similarly for the dean of the arts faculty: ". . . dis-

Johannes Tetzel, from an engraving by Brühl

as the highly dramatized accounts of the events of October 31, 1517, have it, but by the university beadle. So speak the statutes.[14]

5. In an undated letter to Georg Spalatin, advisor to Frederick the Wise, for which the Weimar edition suggests early November as the date, Luther apparently replies to a complaint that although the theses on indulgences are being widely discussed, the court of the prince-elector has received no word about such theses. Luther answers, "I did not want my theses to come into the hands of our illustrious prince-elector or of anyone from the court until the people had received them who are critized in them. They should not think that the theses were ordered or supported by the prince-elector as an attack on the archbishop of Magdeburg; such a rumor—as I hear—is going around." (WBr 1, 118, 9ff.) The people criticized in the theses who were to know of the disputation before Luther's friends learned of it were the bishops, especially Albrecht of Magdeburg and Mainz. Thus Luther explained in his letter to Frederick the Wise on November 21, 1518. (WBr 1, 245) The theses however were mailed to Albrecht on October 31, 1517, at the earliest. Therefore Luther's response to Spalatin, that no one from the court was to learn of the theses before the bishops, effectively excludes a posting of the theses on October 31, 1517.

To grasp this last point we need only to visualize the situation that would have existed before the castle church on the afternoon of October 31, and the day of November 1.

putationes intimet valuis ecclesiarum et collegiorum feria praecedente . . ." *Ibid.*, p. 42. The statutes of the theological faculty speak thus about disputations: "Quilibet Magister praeter examinatcrium publice et solemniter in anno semel disputet. Circulariter autem disputent Magistri omnes secundum ordinem singulis sextis feriis, exceptis vacantiis generalibus, in quibus disputent Baccalaurei ab hora prima usque ad tertiam." *Ibid.*, p. 22. These texts are also to be found in *Urkundenbuch der Universitat Wittenberg*, edited by W. Friedensburg (Magdeburg: 1936), I, 33, 54, and 37, respectively.

[14] "Bidellorum munis esto . . . disputationes, promotiones in scholis publicare et ecclesiarum valuis intimare." *Die Wittenberger Universitäts- und Fakultätsstatuten*, p. 13; Friedensburg, ed., *Urkundenbuch der Universität Wittenberg*, p. 30.

The occasion was the titular feast of this church of All Saints, and the precious collection of relics was on display. For those venerating the relics a great number of indulgences were granted. In addition the Portiuncula indulgence had been granted by Pope Boniface IX to those visiting the castle church on All Saints' Day. This privilege was seldom granted and usually reserved to Franciscan churches. The size of the crowds drawn to the church is indicated by the fact that the confessional faculties for the pastor and eight regular confessors could on All Saints' Day be extended to as many priests as were needed.[15]

In such a situation even the Latin of Luther's theses would not have prevented a scene had they been posted on the church door. For these theses also called in question the pious commerce of the indulgences being offered there that day. Someone from Frederick's court would have learned at least the general intent of the theses, even though Frederick himself was not then in Wittenberg. Further, this situation in and about the church that day would—if the theses were posted—make incredible Luther's frequent assertions that he did not intend to make his theses public, but that he circulated them among only learned men and his educated friends.[16]

Finally, with the Church of All Saints being so filled with visitors on November 1, the suggestion appears ridiculous that a public disputation was planned in the church that day, as Johannes Luther and others contended.[17]

6. Luther circulated his theses in handwritten copies. No

[15] P. Kalkoff, *Forschungen zu Luthers römischen Prozess* (Rome: 1905), p. 63. See also Kalkoff's *Ablass- und Reliquienverehrung an der Schlosskirche zu Wittenberg* (Gotha: 1907), p. 7. Special indulgences could be gained "*a primis vesperis usque ad secundas inclusive,*" therefore on the afternoon of October 31. The privilege regarding confessors came into effect two days earlier. *Ibid.*, p. 94. According to the *Wittemberger Heiligthumsbuch* (see above, p. 26, n. 33) the Portiuncula indulgence could be gained two days before and two days after the Day of All Saints.

[16] See above, p. 79, n. 7.

[17] J. Luther, *Vorbereitung und Verbreitung von M. Luthers 95 Thesen* (Berlin-Leipzig: 1933), p. 9. See also Honselmann, *Urfassung und Drucke*, pp. 24f.

Wittenberg printing of them has come to light, nor can such a printing be proved. The supposition of an original printing in Wittenberg[18] rests on uncritical acceptance of the unproved posting of the theses on October 31 or November 1, 1517. J. K. F. Knaake, editor of the theses in the first volume of the Weimar edition, concluded that the three earliest known editions of the theses were each based on handwritten versions. These editions stem from the turn of the years 1517–18: Edition A (from the press of Hieronymus Hölzel in Nürnberg), Edition B (from Jakob Thanner in Leipzig), and Edition C (from Adam Petri in Basel). Even though Hans Volz postulates an original edition in Wittenberg, he does not see this edition but handwritten copies of it as the basis for the three extant editions.[19] Volz apparently supposes that Luther distributed his printed copies, but these were so few and so precious that the recipients did not pass them on but had copies made for further distribution. Such a hypothesis, however, leaves unexplained why the Wittenberg printer made no further printings but allowed printers in other cities to take over the field.

Most recently Klemens Honselmann's minute investigations led him to conclude that three further printed editions of the theses were based as well on handwritten copies. These are the theses given in the *Resolutiones* (1518), and in the two collections of Luther's disputation theses brought out by Me-

[18] This hypothesis was first proposed by Clemen (*Luthers Werke in Auswahl* [Bonn: 1912], I, 2), and then taken up by J. Luther (*Vorbereitung und Verbreitung*, pp. 11ff.) Köstlin-Kawerau, *Martin Luther* (5th ed.; Berlin: 1903), speak mistakenly of the Nürnberg printing in placard form as the "original printing" of the theses. Aland also supposes that Luther had the theses printed before October 31. "Der Thesenanschlag fand—und zwar am 31. Oktober 1517—statt," p. 693. Volz believes Luther undoubtedly had his theses printed (*Martin Luthers Thesenanschlag*, p. 44), and then posted them in the form of a placard which has since been lost. Volz argues for the placard from the expressions "*schedula disputatoria*" (W 1, 528, 24) and "*disputationis scedulam*" (W 54, 180, 17). "Der Thesenanschlag fand—und zwar wahrscheinlich am 1. November—statt," p. 684. "*Schedula*" however could just as well be a handwritten list of theses. Others find no evidence for an original printing in Wittenberg. On this question, see especially Honselmann, *Urfassung und Drucke*, pp. 17–29.

[19] *Martin Luthers Thesenanschlag und dessen Vorgeschichte*, pp. 44, 134f.

lanchthon in 1530 and by Luther himself in 1538. The same holds for the version of the theses given by the Roman theologian Silvester Prierias in his *Dialogus* against Luther of June 1518. Honselmann further maintains that Luther himself made these handwritten copies, since the variants between them could hardly be from a copyist's mistakes, but are rather the corrections an author would make in consciously improving his own text as he copied it.[20] These conclusions serve to confirm Luther's own account of the way he circulated his theses.[21]

7. According to Honselmann, Luther waited until late December before overcoming his reserve and distributing the handwritten copies of his theses. Honselmann reached this conclusion partly from his investigation of the text of the theses given by Prierias in his *Dialogus* from June 1518. Honselmann agrees with J. K. F. Knaake (cf. W 1, 232) that these are the theses of October 31, sent first to Archbishop Albrecht and then on to Rome, where they came into the hands of Prierias, the *Magister sacri Palatii*, in his function as censor of books. In the *Dialogus* Prierias gives a shorter text of the theses, omitting theses 92 and 93 of our modern editions. Honselmann maintains that Prierias did not have these two theses, since Luther composed them only later. They were Luther's retort to the theses written by the Frankfurt on the Oder professor Konrad Wimpina for defense by his student Johannes Tetzel on the occasion of the latter's reception of the licentiate in theology.[22]

Luther's theses read as follows:

> 92. Away then with all those prophets who say to the people of Christ, "Peace, peace!" and there is no peace.
> 93. Blessed be all those prophets who say to the people of Christ, "Cross, cross!" and there is no cross.[23]

[20] Honselmann, *Urfassung und Drucke*, pp. 50, 64.

[21] See especially Luther's letter to Scheurl, March 5, 1518, WBr 1, 152, 2ff. and the other remarks given above, p. 79, n. 7.

[22] Honselmann, *Urfassung und Drucke*, p. 58.

[23] LW 31, 33 (C. M. Jacobs and Harold J. Grimm).

According to Honselmann these two theses are directed against the following theses from Wimpina-Tetzel:

93. Those who have confessed, who are contrite and have been forgiven, have attained through the remission of all satisfactory punishments to peace, peace.
94. But the remains of sin are still present to incline and induce to a fall.
95. Therefore, he who received forgiveness has peace, peace as to the punishments for what is past. But there remains the cross, the cross of guarding against sin in the future. Whoever denies this lacks insight, and is caught in error and misunderstanding.[24]

From this latter text there is no reason why the three theses from Wimpina-Tetzel were not formulted in opposition to corresponding theses of Luther's, as is the case with the remainder of Wimpina's theses. In fact there is very good evidence for this since these ideas can be found even earlier in Luther's works. On July 23, 1516, Luther wrote to Michael Dressel, the Augustinian prior in Neustadt on the Orla, as follows:

Therefore it is not he whom no one disturbs who has had peace —that is the world's peace—but he who is troubled on every side and who bears all quietly and joyfully. You say with Israel (Jer. 6:14; Ezra 13:10) "Peace, peace," and there is no peace. Cry rather with Christ, "Cross, cross!" And then there is no cross. For, when you can joyfully say, "Blessed cross, of all kinds of wood there is none to compare with you," then the cross is no longer a cross.[25]

Even Honselmann refers explicitly to this letter. Prierias could have simply omitted a response to these theses of Luther's. He says explicitly at the end of the *Dialogus:* "This then, Martin, is what I offer in answer to your theses, except for

[24] The original text of the Wimpina-Tetzel theses is given by Paulus, *Johann Tetzel der Ablassprediger*, pp. 171–80, and by Köhler, *Dokumente zum Ablassstreit*, pp. 128–43.

[25] WBr 1, 47, 31ff. Translation based on Currie, ed., *The Letters of Martin Luther* (London: 1908), p. 10.

some untenable things you say which I omitted at the end."[26] Otherwise, it could be that Luther added the two theses before circulating his theses during November.

In addition, there are serious problems with Honselmann's chronology, especially in arguing that Wimpina's theses reached Luther in the middle of December, more than a month before they were defended by Tetzel on January 20, 1518.[27] This means that Luther would have immediately emended his theses in answer to Wimpina and then sent copies on to Nürnberg and Basel where they appeared in print before the end of 1517.

Further, Luther's remark in *Wider Hans Worst.* "Thus my theses went out against Tetzel's articles," (W 51, 540) does not prove that they were directed against Wimpina-Teztel's antitheses. This can just as well be a reference to Tetzel's sermons on indulgences, for Luther had written just a few lines earlier, "Now I recall how Tetzel preached his horrible and shocking articles, of which I will list a few." (W 51, 539, 12f.) Thus, it seems to me that Honselmann's argumentation goes beyond the evidence.

8. The actual course of events would be approximately as follows: Luther wrote to the bishops, among others to Archbishop Albrecht of Magdeburg and Mainz on October 31, 1517, and then waited for an answer from them. When no answer arrived, or when someone sought to divert him without any serious attention to his call for reform,[28] then Luther circulated his theses among his friends and learned acquain-

[26] "Haec ergo sunt, Martine, quae ad conclusiones tuas respondenda occurrerunt, posthabitis in fine quibusdam sanis, quae loqueris." Given by Aland, *Martin Luthers 95 Thesen* (Hamburg: 1965), p. 102. Honselmann stresses that his theory is but one of a number of possible ones. *Urfassung und Drucke*, p. 60, n. 15.

[27] Paulus maintained that the idea that the Wimpina-Tetzel theses were printed in 1517 was unfounded. *Johann Tetzel*, p. 170. Honselmann argues against this, on the basis of the date given in Luther's *Opera Omnia* (Wittenberg: 1545), I, fol. 96bff. *Urfassung und Drucke*, p. 117.

[28] See Luther's report on the reaction of the bishop of Brandenburg, pp. 58–59, above.

tances. The first example we have of this is the letter to Johannes Lang on November 11, 1517. Many of those receiving the theses would have reacted as did Johannes Fleck, the guardian of a Franciscan friary, who upon seeing the theses exclaimed to his fellow Franciscans, "Here's the man we've been waiting for!" and then wrote Luther an enthusiastic letter.[29]

Many who received the theses passed them on to others. For example, Christoph Scheurl, a lawyer in Nürnberg, received them from Ulrich von Dinstedt, a canon of the castle church in Wittenberg. On January 5, 1518, Scheurl wrote in acknowledgment: "I am most grateful to have received Martin's theses. Friends here have translated them and we think highly of them."[30] Later Scheurl indirectly confirmed that he had received a handwritten copy of the theses. He wrote in his *History of Christianity* in 1528: "Luther composed ninety-five theses on indulgences and sent them to the other doctors. He certainly did not want them to circulate more widely, for they were only handwritten. Neither did he want to defend them all, but only discuss them and thus learn the opinion of others about them. . . . But an extraordinary and unheard of thing took place, as they were frequently copied and sent all over Germany as something new and unusual."[31]

We may suppose that the copy sent by Ulrich von Dinstedt to Scheurl served as the basis of the extant Nürnberg Edition A. With this printing Scheurl was able to forward copies to various learned friends, e.g., to Konrad Peutinger on January 5, 1518,[32] and to Johannes Eck in Ingolstadt and to

[29] WBr 5, 177, n. 5480.

[30] *Chr. Scheurl's Briefbuch*, edited by Freiherr von Soden and Knaake (Potsdam: 1872 and by reprint, Aalen: 1962), II, 42, n. 158. See Volz, *Martin Luthers Thesenanschlag*, p. 131. Clemen falsely supposed that the theses forwarded by Scheurl on November 5 to Truchsess, Leib, and Eck were the ninety-five indulgence theses. WBr 1, 116, n. 9. See on this Volz, *Martin Luthers Thesenanschlag*, pp. 114f.

[31] Knaake, ed., *Geschichtsbuch der Christenheit* in *Jahrbücher des deutschen Reiches und deutschen Kirche im Zeitalter der Reformation*, I, 112.

[32] *Briefbuch*, II, 40, n. 156.

others. On January 8, Scheurl reported to Caspar Güttel, an Augustinian in Eisleben, "I am gradually ensuring for Dr. M. Luther the friendship of illustrious men. Pirkheimer, A. Tucher, and Wenzeslaus are both amazed and delighted with his theses. C. Nutzel translated them into German, and I sent them on to Augsburg and Ingolstadt."[33]

About the same time, Scheurl sent Luther printed copies of the theses in both Latin and German. Apparently, in his covering letter he expressed his disappointment in not receiving the theses from Luther himself. Luther answered in his own defense on March 5, 1518:

> You are surprised that I did not send them to you. But I did not want to circulate them widely. I only intended to submit them to a few close friends for discussion, and if they disapproved of the theses, to suppress them. I wanted to publish them, only if they met with approval. But now they are being printed and spread everywhere far beyond my expectation, a result that I regret. It is not that I am against telling the people the truth, in fact that is alone what I want, but this is not the proper way to instruct the people. For I have doubts about some of the theses, and others I would have put much differently and more cogently, and some I would have omitted, had I known what was to come. Still, the spread of my theses shows what people everywhere really think of indulgences, although they conceal their thoughts "out of fear of the Jews." Therefore, I had to write out proofs for my theses, but I do not yet have permission to publish these.[34]

Accordingly, the printing of the theses in late December and early January did not take place at Luther's initiative and was in fact effected without his approval. His own friends presented him, as it were, with an accomplished fact. Nonetheless, he let events take their course, and from the spring of

[33] *Ibid.*, p. 43f. n. 160.

[34] WBr 1, 152, 1ff. Currie, ed., *The Letters of Martin Luther*, p. 23. We gain an insight into Luther's attitude to church authority from the fact that he sent his explanations of the theses to Bishop Hieronymus, his ordinary, and then waited for his approval before publishing them.

1518 onward, i.e., after the various printings appeared, he felt justified in saying that he had issued a public invitation to an oral or written theological discussion of the theses. This is not wholly correct, since it conflicts with Luther's frequent expressions of pained regret at the spread of the theses. However, this does agree with the outward events, since Luther's words in the preface of the theses call for a disputation or at least for written contributions, and the public would suppose that Luther himself had commissioned the printing of the theses.

9. At any rate, Luther asserted after February, 1518, that he had issued a public invitation to a discussion on indulgences. In a letter commonly dated February 13, 1518, he wrote to Bishop Hieronymus in Brandenburg, to whom he had submitted his *Resolutiones* for examination:

> In order to satisfy both sides in the controversy over indulgences, it seemed best neither to agree with nor to oppose anyone, but rather to dispute this important question until the church decided what was to be held. And so I put out a disputation, inviting all publicly and a few learned men of my acquaintance privately, asking them to at least make a written statement of their position.[35] My ideas did not seem to be contrary to scripture, nor to the doctors of the church, nor to church law. (WBr 1, 138, 14ff.)

After a long passage on the necessity of proving one's theological opinions with good reasons and of posing open questions for discussion, Luther continues:

> I called all into the arena, but no one came. Then I saw how my theses were being circulated more widely than I had wished, and that they were being taken as a certain position and not as topics for disputation. Thus I was forced to go against my own wishes and inclinations, and further parade my ignorance and inexperience before the public by bringing out explanations and proofs of my theses. (WBr 1, 139, 46ff.)

[35] "Itaque emisi disputationem, invitans et rogans publice omnes, privatim ut nosti, quosque doctissimos, ut vel per literas suam sententiam aperirent." WBr 1, 138, 17ff. Volz pointed out that all manuscripts read "*ut novi*" in this sentence.

At the end of the letter, Luther emphasizes that it was the audacity and ignorance of people proclaiming their own dreams as the gospel truth that compelled him to overcome his fear and to propose a disputation. If the indulgence preachers, with their threats and their papal bulls, had not been so foolhardy and so outright dumb, "then no one would have heard of me outside my little corner." [36]

Accordingly, Luther asserts that he issued disputation theses and asked for at least written expressions of opinion. This invitation took place in two ways: publicly for all, and privately (i.e., orally or by mail) for his learned acquaintances.

If one knew nothing at all about a supposed posting of the theses, one would think that Luther had his theses printed and then sent some copies privately to his acquaintances. A posting of the theses on the bulletin board of the university—the door of the castle church—fits neither with the phrase "*publice omnes,*" nor with "*privatim doctissimos,*" nor with the invitation for a written contribution. Luther will have it that he appealed to a wider public than that afforded by the university. He expresses this idea when he says that only the noise of the indulgence preachers led him to overcome his fear and call for a disputation. Otherwise, he would have remained in his corner as an unknown professor. Earlier, on September 4, 1517, he spoke of the Wittenberg university as a "corner." [37] With a theses posting in Wittenberg, Luther would still have been "whispering in his corner." (WBr 1, 103, 14)

Further, a posting of the theses is not demanded by Luther's remark that he challenged all to enter the arena but that none came. The arena is not necessarily the disputation hall, as Hans Volz supposed. [38] Luther, like Erasmus, used *arena* when speaking of a literary exchange. For example, in a remark at table, Luther spoke thus of the indulgence controversy: "Soon Silvester [Prierias], the master of the sacred

[36] "Quae nisi tanta esset, nullus me praeter quam angulus meus cognovisset." WBr 1, 140, 77.

[37] See above, p. 77, n. 2.

[38] *Martin Luthers Thesenanschlag und dessen Vorgeschichte*, pp. 108f., n.154.

palace, entered the arena and began roaring at me." (WTr3, 564, n. 3722) Here Luther indicates that Prierias, a court theologian for the pope, was the first to write against him, in the *Dialogus* of June 1518. The only way to do justice to the phrase "*invitans et rogans publice omnes*" is by visualizing a printing of the theses. Since we cannot follow Aland and Volz in postulating an original printing in Wittenberg (for which there is no evidence, as we saw above), then we must see the printings around New Year's in other cities as the basis for Luther's assertion.

One thinks here of the parallel case regarding Luther's appeal to a council on November 28, 1518. On this day, Luther stated his appeal to "a council soon and legitimately to be called in the Holy Spirit" before notaries and witnesses in the Corpus Christi chapel of the Wittenberg parish church. He sent the document to the printer, not however for circulation, but only that copies might be on hand if Luther were excommunicated and exiled. But the sharp-eyed printer began to sell copies of it, as Luther complained (WBr 1, 270, 15 and 280, 6), even before the author received a copy. Luther had therefore not formally made an appeal, but had only prepared to do this. Thus, it was more or less an accident that triggered this act of such great historical significance. And so we can expect that when developments have reached a climax, and Luther shrinks from the decisive step or is hindered by considerations of a diplomatic nature, still he would let others take the fateful step for him. At any rate, he professed agreement with the appeal of November 1518, which he could hardly avoid, and went on to express satisfaction over this turn of events. As he wrote about it to Spalatin on December 20, 1518: "I cannot undo what has now happened." (WBr 1, 281, 12)

Similarly, Luther could judge as his own work and his own responsibility the printing of his theses on indulgences, because he had circulated manuscripts of them and because their preface invited the reader to join in a disputation or at least to give a written opinion on them.

Frederick the Wise, from an engraving of 1524
by Albrecht Dürer in the Museum of Fine Arts, Boston

10. In a letter to Spalatin on February 15, 1518, Luther also speaks of a public invitation to discuss his theses. This would be at approximately the same time as the letter to Bishop Hieronymus which we have just treated. Luther expresses regret that the prince-elector has been drawn into the affair, and according to the rumors going about that Frederick the Wise had incited Luther against his political rival Archbishop Albrecht. Providing he be given safe conduct, Luther is willing to appear for a disputation or for a juridical investigation. But no one should involve the wholly innocent prince in any way in the charge of suspected heresy directed against Luther. Luther concludes with this general remark on his own situation:

> Behold these monstrous men and this people of darkness! They pursue John Reuchlin through three countries to bring him to court against his will. But when I issue an invitation *ante fores* and offer a public challenge, they despise me and whisper off in a corner that which they fear to defend publicly.[39]

Peter Meinhold translates "*ante fores*" in this passage literally as "before the doors," and maintained that this was an unambiguous reference to the posting of the ninety-five theses on the doors of the castle church in Wittenberg. He wrote, "This is an irrefutable witness, not just that Luther issued a public invitation to a disputation, but that he did this by posting his ninety-five theses 'before the doors.' "[40]

The research and discussion concerning the posting of the theses have reached agreement that "*ante fores*" is to be translated "before a wide public."[41] The language of scripture is a

[39] "Vide Monstrosum hominum genus et tenebrarum populum lucis Inimicum. Iohannem Reuchlin ultra tres provincias invenerunt et traxerunt Invitum, Me ante fores Invitantem et rogantem spernunt et in angulis garriunt, quod defendere se non posse vident." WBr 1, 146, 89.

[40] Meinhold, "Luthers Thesenanschlag fand doch statt: Eine Antwort auf die Behauptung eines katholischen Theologen," *Christ und Welt*, XV (August 3, 1962, p. 10.

[41] F. Lau, "Möglich ist auch die Übersetzung 'öffentlich,' " *Lutherische Monatshefte*, I (1962), p. 262. Lohse, "Meinholds Argument gegen Iserloh dürfte sich also nicht aufrecht erhalten lassen," *Luther*, XXXIV (1963), p. 134. Volz, "Erzbischof Albrecht von Mainz und Martin Luthers 95 Thesen," *Jahrbuch der Hessischen kirchengeschichtlichen Vereinigung*, XIII (1962), p. 219, n. 124. Honselmann, *Urfassung und Drucke*, pp. 108f.

first argument for this, where "before the doors" or "at the door" (*in foribus* or *in porta*) means "publicly" or "in conversation with others." (See, for example, Prov. 1:21; 8:3; Ps. 127:5; Amos 5:15; etc.) In this letter to Spalatin Luther opposes "*ante fores*" and "*in angulis*," just as he contrasted "*publice*" and "*in angulum*" in his letter to Lang on September 4, 1517. (See WBr 1, 103, 10) Thus Luther's phrasing in writing to Spalatin, "*me ante fores invitantem et rogantem*," has the same meaning as "*invitans et rogans publice omnes*" in the letter to Bishop Hieronymus.

Since Luther appears to have felt that he was living off in a corner in Wittenberg, a posting of the theses in the university would not suffice to verify Luther's description of his invitation as having been made "*publice*" and "*ante fores.*" It would also be strange if Luther had made this juxtaposition in the letter to Spalatin: first, Luther regrets that rumors were involving the prince-elector in his case, but then he refers (so it is argued) to a public invitation issued by Luther's theses being posted on the door of Frederick's own castle church. One can make sense out of Luther's different argumentation in the two letters to Spalatin (November 1517 and February 15, 1518) only by supposing that in the time between the two letters the theses have become known in printed versions.

Thus, the phrases "*invitans publice*" and "*ante fores*" used as a principal argument by the defenders of the posting of the theses turn out to be no argument at all for a posting on October 31 or November 1. Far too much evidence rules this out. If one, however, still feels the need of postulating such a posting, then it should be dated in mid-November, at about the time Luther sent his theses to Johannes Lang.

VII. BUT STILL THE REFORMATION BEGAN ON OCTOBER 31, 1517

OUR INVESTIGATION of the sources and the reports concerning October 31, 1517, compels us to conclude that the drama of that day was notably less than what we would suppose from the jubilee celebrations which have been held since 1617 and from the Reformation Day festivals since their inception in 1668. In fact the sources rule out a public posting of the ninety-five theses.

Although October 31, 1517, lacked outward drama it was nevertheless a day of decisive importance. It is the day on which the Reformation began, not because Martin Luther posted his ninety-five theses on the door of the castle church in Wittenberg, but because on this day Luther approached the competent church authorities with his pressing call for reform. On this day he presented them with his theses and the request that they call a halt to the unworthy activities of the indulgence preachers. When the bishops did not respond, or when they sought merely to divert him, Luther circulated his theses privately. The theses spread quickly and were printed in Nürnberg, Leipzig, and Basel. Suddenly they were echoing throughout Germany and beyond its borders in a way that Luther neither foresaw nor intended. The protest that Luther registered before Archbishop Albrecht and the inclusion of the theses with the letter eventually led to the Roman investigation of Luther's works.

Some will surely want to object: Is it not actually of minor importance whether Luther posted his theses in Wittenberg or not? I would answer that it is of more than minor importance. For October 31 was a day on which the castle church was crowded with pilgrims taking advantage of the titular feast of All Saints. Luther's theses on the door would have constituted a public protest. If Luther made such a scene on the same day that he composed his letter to Archbishop Albrecht, then his letter loses its credibility, even when we take into account its excessive protestations of submissiveness and humility as conventions of the time.[1]

Above all, if Luther did post his theses, then for the rest of his life he knowingly gave a false account of these events by asserting that he only circulated his theses after the bishops failed to act.

If the theses were not posted on October 31, 1517, then it becomes all the more clear that Luther did not rush headlong toward a break with the church. Rather, as Joseph Lortz has never tired of repeating,[2] and as Luther himself stressed,[3] he started the Reformation quite unintentionally. In the preface to an edition of his theses in 1538 Luther gave a detailed picture of the situation in 1517. It is as if he wanted to warn the Protestant world against dramatizing the start of the Reformation with false heroics. First he stresses how weak, reticent, and unsure he was; then he tells of his efforts to contact church authorities. This is something he knows his readers cannot appreciate, since they have grown used to impudent attacks on the broken authority of the pope. Luther wrote:

> I was alone and through poor judgment (*per imprudentiam*) I fell into this controversy. . . . I was a most miserable little monk, more a corpse than a man, and was I to oppose the pope's

[1] Meissinger was more harsh in judging this part of Luther's letter to Albrecht, *Der katholische Luther*, p. 159.

[2] See Lortz, *The Reformation: A Problem for Today*. Translated by John C. Dwyer, S. J. (Westminster, Md.: 1964), pp. 115f.

[3] For example: "In negotium evangelii insciens a Deo coniectus sum. Quodsi praevidissem ea, quae nunc expertus sum, nullo modo passus fuissem me adigere . . ." WTr 1, 601, n. 1206. Luther wrote to Pope Leo X in May 1518: ". . . invitus venio in publicum periculosissimumque ac varium hominum iudicium, praesertim ego indoctus, stupidus ingenio, vacuus eruditione." W 1, 529, 4ff.

> exalted majesty? . . . What my heart suffered in those first two years, and how great was my quite genuine humility—and near despair! How little of all this those knew who later took up the attack against the pope's injured majesty. And though they had not written these verses (to quote Vergil), they received the honors. But this I do not regret.
>
> But when they were mere onlookers letting me face the danger, then I was neither happy, confident, nor sure of myself. I was then ignorant of much that I now know. In fact, I had no inkling what indulgences were, just as no one among the papists knew anything about them. They were only honored by reason of tradition and custom. My disputation was not aimed at abolishing indulgences, but only to find out what they really were, since I had some idea what they were not. And when the speechless and deceased teachers, i.e., the books of the theologians and jurists, did not satisfy me, I decided to consult the living. I wanted to hear the church of God, and if the Holy Spirit could still speak in her, I hoped that she might have pity on my ignorance and for the benefit of all say clearly what indulgences were. And many good men praised my theses.[4]

If Luther did turn first to the competent bishops with his protest, or better, with his earnest plea for reform, and if he did give them time to react as their pastoral responsibilities called for, then it is the bishops who clearly were more responsible for the consequences. If Luther did allow the bishops time to answer his request then he was sincere in begging the archbishop to remove the scandal before disgrace came upon him and upon the church.

Further, there was clearly a real opportunity that Luther's challenge could be directed to the reform of the church, instead of leading to a break with the church. But such reform would have demanded of the bishops far greater religious substance and a far more lively priestly spirit than they showed. The deficiencies that come to light here, precisely when the bishops were called on to act as theologians and pastors, cannot be rated too highly when we seek to determine

[4] W 39I, 6, 9–32.

the causes of the Reformation. These deficiencies had far more serious consequences than did the failures in personal morality that we usually connect with the "bad popes" and concubinous priests on the eve of the Reformation. Archbishop Albrecht showed on other occasions as well how indifferent he was to theological questions, and how fully incapable he was of comprehending their often wideranging religious significance. For example, he expressed his displeasure over the momentous Leipzig debate of 1519 where famous professors were, as he saw it, crossing swords over minor points of no interest for true Christian men.[5] This same Albrecht sent sizable gifts of money to Luther on the occasion of his marriage in 1525[6] and to Melanchthon after the latter had sent him a copy of his commentary on Romans in 1532.[7]

A whole series of objections might arise here: Do not the indulgence theses themselves mark the break with the church? Do they not attack the very foundations of the church of that day? Or, as Heinrich Bornkamm wrote, do they not decisively pull the ground from under the Catholic conception of penance?[8] Was a reform of the church of that day at all possible by renewal from within? Is not the Luther of the ninety-five theses already a revolutionary on his way inevitably to the Reformation as a division of the church?

[5] See his remarks, WBr 2, 54, 26f.

[6] WTr 3, 154, n. 3038b; WBr 4, 56f. On this see Volz, "Erzbischof Albrecht von Mainz," p. 227, n. 157.

[7] *Corpus Reformatorum*, II, col. 629. See also WTr 5, 690, n. 6486, and WTr 4, 640, n. 5067. Kalkoff judged Albrecht to be effete, luxury loving, and wholly uninterested in theology and the duties of his office. *Ulrich von Hutten und die Reformation* (Leipzig: 1920), p. 51. Volz demurred in his 1962 article on Albrecht and Luther, urging that this was not just in view of the high office Albrecht held. But this is beside the point, especially since Albrecht came into high office not on his merits but because of his willingness to pay the pallium and dispensation fees out of his own pocket. The material that Volz presents does not change our judgment on Albrecht as an archbishop, though as a renaissance prince he is quite impressive. He is perhaps somewhat excused by the generally low quality of the bishops of his day, but still he and his confreres give us an important insight into the causes of the Reformation.

[8] Heinrich Bornkamm, "The World-historical Significance of the 95 Theses,' in *Luther's World of Thought* (St. Louis: 1958), p. 46.

Our first question must be whether Luther's indulgence theses deny any binding doctrines of the church in his day. And even if this be true, we cannot immediately brand the Luther of late 1517 a heretic. This would be justified only if he became aware of holding something opposed to the teaching of the church and then remained adamant in the face of correction. It is especially important to recall this in view of Luther's repeated assertions that the theses do not express his own position, but that much in them is doubtful, that some points he would reject, and no single one out of all of them would he stubbornly maintain.[9]

The theses begin, "When our Lord and teacher Jesus Christ said 'Do penance,' he meant that the whole life of the faithful should be one of penance." This is neither a reference to the sacrament of penance (2), nor to interior penance alone, since the latter is of no worth "unless it issue in different outward acts of mortification." (3) "Therefore penance remains as long as hatred of self remains (i.e., true inner penance), namely until one enters the kingdom of heaven." (4) Here we see the same concern we saw in Luther's earlier statements on indulgences: The faithful must not doze off in false security about their salvation. Rather, "Christians should be exhorted to follow Christ, their head, in bearing penance, death and hell itself." (94, see also theses 92–95) "True contrition seeks and loves penances." (40) But indulgences teach people to flee penances.

No one knows whether his sorrow be genuine (30), and those truly gaining remission of punishment are as rare as those who are truly repentant, that is quite rare. (31)

The indulgence preachers, by their extravagant and immoderate words (72), commend indulgences out of all proportion to their real worth (24, 73–80) and thereby lend support to a false sense of peace. (95) In this situation the will to repent and to do penance grows slack. (39–40) Later, Luther made this same point in the *Resolutiones:* "Danger here! See

[9] See above, p. 82, n. 11.

how they proclaim indulgences dead against the truth of the cross and the fear of God." (W 1, 601, 34f.)

Luther did not simply reject indulgences. In fact, he wrote, "Let him be anathema and accursed who speaks against the apostolic character of these indulgences." (71) But a man must not put his trust in them. (32, 49, 52) The works of charity and prayer rank far ahead of indulgences. (41–45, 48) In an indulgence the pope has neither the will nor the power to remit punishments other than those he or canon law has imposed. (5) Such punishments can be imposed only on the living. (8) "In earlier times ecclesiastical penances were not imposed after, but before granting absolution; these were tests of genuine sorrow for sin." (12) If the pope can only remit the penances he has imposed (20), then the preachers are in error, when they say that papal indulgences free a person from all guilt and punishment. (21) We saw how the "*Instructio summaria*" and the indulgence preachers gave the impression that one gains forgiveness of sins and comes to share in the spiritual goods of Christ and the church by way of indulgences. Luther counters that every truly contrite Christian attains full remission of guilt and penance (36) and shares in the spiritual goods of Christ and the church even without an indulgence. (37)

The "treasury of the church" by which the pope grants indulgences is neither sufficiently explained, nor enough known among Christ's people. (56) What is in this treasury? Obviously not temporal riches. (57) But also not the merits of Christ and his saints, since even without the pope's intervention "these merits are constantly bringing grace to the inner man and producing the cross, death, and hell itself for the outer man." (58) Luther will not bind the grace giving powers of Christ to the authority of the pope. But, on the other hand, he will not at all exclude the latter. He goes on to indicate what this treasury is: "the keys of the church, bestowed by Christ's merits." (60) But the true treasure of the church is the most holy gospel of the glory and grace of God. (62) Therefore, they are enemies of Christ who prohibit the word of God while the indulgence is being preached (as the *instructio* did).[10] (53–55) Theses 14–19 bring out the uncertainty of theological statements about the condition of the souls in purgatory. In any case, indulgences for the departed are granted *per modum suffragii* (26), and so one may not speak of an infallible effect here. (27) "The intercession offered by the church depends on God's decision." (28) Then too, no one can know whether all the souls in purgatory want to be released. (29) All these theses can be understood as justified criticism of the abuses in indulgence practices and as a contribution to a discussion of open questions among theologians.

Even Luther's conception of the declarative nature of absolution was in line with the nominalist theology of the day. Accordingly, the pope remits guilt only in the sense that he declares and confirms that this has been forgiven by God. (6, 38) By this theory even sacramental absolution does not itself remove guilt and eternal punishment but only indicates the remission that has already taken place.[11]

Luther stresses the intention of going to confession as a condition of forgiveness by God. (7, 38) He even acknowledges that the pope has the right to reserve sins with effect before God. (6) As in his treatise on indulgences, he limits indulgences to the remission of canonical punishments (5, 11, 20, 21, 33), and says nothing about any correspondence between ecclesiastical satisfaction and satisfaction imposed by God. However, as he explained his position on precisely this point, he repeatedly said that he was disputing, not asserting, and that he would gladly accept correction on this point.[12]

Luther knows that he is opposing theologians like St. Thomas and St. Bonaventure. He also knows that he is not

[10] Köhler, *Dokumente zum Ablassstreit*, p. 107, l. 25.

[11] Poschmann, *Penance and the Annointing of the Sick*, p. 192.

[12] The explanation of Thesis 5 begins, "*Hanc disputo et doceri humiliter peto* . . ." W 1, 534, 22. For Thesis 20: "*Hanc disputo, nondum pertinaciter assero.*" W 1, 567, 29. But in the explanation of Thesis 36 Luther calls it a monstrosity to teach that canonical punishments serve to declare punishments imposed by God. W 1, 592, 38ff.

the first, nor is he the only one to question their teachings. Nothing in scripture or canon law is against him, and the church has made no binding decision in this question. (W 1, 568, 13ff.) Luther is convinced that he is arguing within an area of free theological opinion. Our knowledge of the theological situation at the end of the fifteenth century would confirm this. Further, Luther did submit his *Resolutiones*, i.e., the explanations of his theses, to his ordinary, the bishop of Brandenburg, and received from him permission for publication. (See WBr 1, 164)

As we indicated in our first chapter, contemporary Catholic theology also leans toward seeing an indulgence as a jurisdictional act regarding the remission of ecclesiastical penances only. The practice of the church seems to go against St. Thomas on this point, indicating that an indulgence for the living also works *per modum suffragii* and is the church's petition before God for a remission of temporal punishment which then depends on God's acceptance for its effectiveness.[13]

Still, a truly historical judgment on the theses will not consider their precise wording only. We must further ask in what direction they are tending and what development is already immanent in them. Luther's theses can only be understood in the context of late medieval nominalism. This theology had already made a broad separation of divine and human activity in the church. For God, actions in the church were only occasions for his saving action, with no true involvement of the latter in the former. Regarding penance and the remission of punishment, Luther simply carries the nominalist separation of the ecclesiastical and the divine to the extreme in that he denies that ecclesiastical penances and their remission even have an interpretative relation to the penance required by or remitted by God. I see here one root of Luther's impending denial of the hierarchical priesthood established by God in the church.

The theological consequences of the ninety-five theses

[13] Poschmann, *Penance and the Annointing of the Sick*, pp. 230ff.

were not immediately effective. The secret of their wide circulation and their electrifying effect was that they voiced a popular polemic. Here Luther touched on questions, complaints, and resentments that had long been smouldering and had often been expressed already. Luther made himself the spokesman for those whose hopes for reform had often been disappointed in a period of widespread dissatisfaction.

Theses 81–90 list the pointed questions the laity ask about indulgences. If the pope can, as he claims, free souls from purgatory, why then does he not do this out of Christian charity, instead of demanding money as a condition? Why does he not forget his building project and simply empty purgatory? (82) If indulgences are so salutary for the living, why does the pope grant them to the faithful but once a day and not a hundred times? (88) If the pope is more intent on helping souls toward salvation than in obtaining money, why is it that he makes new grants and suspends earlier confessional letters and indulgences which are just as effective? (89) If indulgences are so certain, and if it is wrong to pray for people already saved, why are anniversary masses for the dead still celebrated? Why is the money set aside for these masses not returned? (83) Why does the pope not build St. Peter's out of his own huge wealth, instead of with the money of the poor? (86) These are serious and conscientious questions posed by laymen. If they are merely beaten down by authority, instead of being met with good reasons, then the church and the pope will be open to the ridicule of their enemies. This will only increase the misery of the Christian people. (90)

Here Luther's theses brought thoughts out into the open that all had more or less consciously found troublesome. Many would have greeted the theses like the Franciscan Johannes Fleck with the exclamation, "Here's the man we've been waiting for!" (WTr 5, 177, n. 5480) A good index to their timeliness is the welcome given them by men such as Johannes Cochläus, Hieronymus Emser, and Duke George of Saxony who later were outspoken opponents of Luther. The duke's advisor, Caesar Pflug, reported that Bishop Adolf of Merseburg remarked that Luther's theses should be publicly posted in every town to warn the poor against Tetzel's fraud.[14] In 1521 the Franciscan confessor of Emperor Charles V, Glapion, told the Saxon chancellor, Brück, that Luther's first intervention on indulgences, i.e., the theses and *Resolutiones*, was quite praiseworthy. In fact only a very few learned men would not have agreed with his initial position.[15]

The rapid dissemination of his theses was for Luther proof that he had written what many were thinking but, as in John 7:13, they would not speak out openly "out of fear of the Jews." (WBr 1, 152, 17)

Luther regretted the spread of the theses, since they were not meant for the public, but only for a few learned men. Furthermore, the theses contained a number of doubtful points.[16] Therefore he rushed the "Sermon on Indulgences and Grace" into print in March 1518 (W 1, 239–46) as a popular presentation of his basic point on indulgences, and he wrote the *Resolutiones* (W 1, 526–628 and LW 31, 83–252) as an extensive theological explanation of the theses. The *Resolutiones*, although finished in February, appeared only in August 1518, since the bishop of Brandenburg took some time to give his approval for publication. In this case Luther waited to hear from the bishop, something he had not done earlier, if he actually posted his theses on October 31, 1517.[17]

In the letter to the pope which Luther wrote in late May 1518 and had printed with the *Resolutiones* he said, "Therefore, Most Holy Father, I kneel at your feet and give myself over to you with all that I am and have." (W 1, 529, 23f.)

[14] Gess, ed., *Akten und Briefe zur Kirchenpolitik Herzog Georgs von Sachsen*, I, 29.
[15] *Deutsche Reichstagsakten*, II, 486.
[16] Luther wrote this to Scheurl on March 5, 1518, WBr 1, 152, 7ff.
[17] In his letter of March 5, 1518, Luther wrote ". . . *quas tamen nondum licuit edere, quia reverendus et gratiosus Dominus Episcopus Brandenburgensis, cuius iudicium consului in hac re, multum impeditus tam diu me retardat.*" WBr 1, 152, 18ff. On April 4, Luther reported in a letter to Spalatin that the bishop had answered and given permission for the publication of the explanations.

In a declaration that prefaces the *Resolutiones*, Luther wrote:

> First, I testify that I desire to say or maintain absolutely nothing except, first of all, what is in the Holy Scriptures and can be maintained from them; and then what is in and from the writings of the church fathers and is accepted by the Roman church and preserved both in the canons and the papal decrees.

Thus, Luther refused to be bound by mere theological opinion. He concluded:

> From this declaration I believe that it is made sufficiently clear that I can err, but also that I shall not be considered a heretic for that reason no matter how much those who think and wish differently should rage or be consumed with anger.[18]

These prefatory statements accompanying the explanations of the theses have been singled out for a remarkable combination of loyal submissiveness, prophetic sense of mission, and an almost arrogant conviction of their cause. Meissinger saw here the maneuverings of a chess expert.[19] This does not strike me as an adequate analysis. I see rather the genuine possibility of keeping Luther within the church. But for this to have happened the bishops who were involved, and the pope himself, would have to have matched Luther in religious substance and in pastoral earnestness. It was not just a cheap evasion when Luther repeated again and again in 1517 and 1518 that he felt bound only by teachings of the church and not by theological opinions, even if these came from St. Thomas or St. Bonaventure.[20] The binding declaration Luther sought from the church came in Leo X's doctrinal constitution on indulgences, "*Cum postquam*" (DS 1447ff.), on November 9, 1518. This was based on a text prepared by Cardinal Cajetan, and was published by him on December 13, 1518, in Linz on the Danube in what is now Austria.

The papal constitution declares that the pope by reason

[18] W 1, 529, 33–530, 12. LW 31, 83 (Carl M. Folkemer).
[19] *Der katholische Luther*, p. 162.
[20] W 1, 530, 4f.

of the power of the keys can through indulgences remit punishments for sin by applying the merits of Christ and the saints. The living receive this remission as an absolution and the departed by way of intercession. The constitution was quite reticent and sparing in laying down binding doctrine. This contrasts notably with the manner of the indulgence preachers and Luther's attackers. Cajetan himself felt compelled in a treatise on indulgences on November 20, 1519, to criticize preachers who were publicizing their private opinions as the doctrine of the church.[21]

Tetzel's disputation in Frankfurt on the Oder in January 1518 gives a good example of the extent of this thoughtless identification of personal theological opinion with dogma, and the consequent branding of an opponent as a heretic. Tetzel's thesis 42 asserts that it is "Christian dogma" that one need not be in the state of grace to gain a plenary indulgence for the departed[22]—a thesis Luther found repulsive and which Catholic theologians today unanimously reject.

This arbitrary proclamation of dogma in open theological questions was surely one of the most dangerous forms of the "theological confusion" of the time. Added to this was the shocking lack of religious earnestness evident in the first responses to Luther's intervention.

In his thirty-fourth thesis Tetzel lightly defended the conception that underlay the sardonic couplet, "When the coin in the basket clings, then the soul from the fire springs." In fact Tetzel maintained that the soul would be freed even more quickly, since a spirit needed no time to move from purgatory to heaven, while the coin needed time for falling into the basket.[23]

Silvester Prierias, the papal court theologian, exceeded his fellow Dominican Tetzel in frivolity. For him, a preacher

[21] See his indulgence treatise of November 20, 1519, *Opuscula omnia* (Lyon: 1562), p. 105a.

[22] Paulus, *Johann Tetzel der Ablassprediger*, p. 175.

[23] "Quisquis ergo dicit, non citius posse animam evolare, quam in fundo cistae denarius possit tinnire, errat." *Ibid.*, pp. 143f., 174.

maintaining the doctrines attacked by Luther is much like a cook adding seasoning to make a dish more appealing.[24] Here we see the same lack of religious earnestness and pastoral awareness that marked the bishops' reaction to the theses.

This lack of theological competence and of apostolic concern was all the more freighted with consequences, in the face of Martin Luther's zeal for the glory of God and the salvation of souls in 1517–18. There was a real chance to channel his zeal toward renewal of the church from within.

In this context it does seem important whether Luther actually posted his theses for the benefit of the crowds streaming into the Church of All Saints in Wittenberg. It is important whether he made such a scene or whether he simply presented his ninety-five theses to the bishops and to some learned friends. From the former he sought the suppression of practical abuses, and from the latter the clarification of open theological questions.

I, for one, feel compelled to judge Luther's posting of the ninety-five theses a legend. With this legend removed it is much clearer to what a great extent the theological and pastoral failures of the bishops set the scene for Luther to begin the divisive Reformation we know, instead of bringing reform from within the church.

[24] *Dialogus*, B 1[a]; See also Paulus, *Johann Tetzel*, p. 147.

BIBLIOGRAPHY

Aland, K. "Der 31. Oktober gilt zu Recht als der Tag des Thesenanschlags Martin Luthers," *Deutsches Pfarrerblatt*, LVIII (1958), 241–5.

———. "Luthers Thesenanschlag: Tatsache oder Legende?" *Deutsches Pfarrerblatt*, LXII (1962), 241–4.

———. "Der Thesenanschlag fand—und zwar wahrscheinlich am 31. Oktober 1517—statt," *Geschichte in Wissenschaft und Unterricht*, XVI (1965), 686–94.

———. *Martin Luthers 95 Thesen. Mit den dazugehörigen Dokumenten aus der Geschichte der Reformation.* Hamburg: 1965.

Boehmer, H. *Der junge Luther*. 4th ed., revised by Heinrich Bornkamm. Stuttgart: 1951. ET: *Martin Luther—Road to Reformation.* Translated by John W. Doberstein and Theodore G. Tappert. London: 1957.

Friedensburg, W. *Urkundenbuch der Universität Wittenberg*, Vol. I: 1502–1611. Magdeburg: 1926.

Gess, F. *Akten und Briefe zur Kirchenpolitik Herzog Georgs von Sachsen*, Vol. I: 1517–1524. Leipzig: 1905.

———. "Luthers Thesen und Herzog Georg von Sachsen," *Zeitschrift für Kirchengeschichte*, IX (1888), 590f.

Gröne, V. *Tetzel und Luther*, 2nd ed. Soest: 1860.

Harms, K. "Luthers Thesenanschlag," *Deutsches Pfarrerblatt*, LXIII (1963), 519f.

Haussleiter, J. *Die Universität Wittenberg vor dem Eintritt Luthers.* Leipzig: 1903.

Höss, I. "Diskussion über Luthers Thesenanschlag—Bericht," *Geschichte in Wissenschaft und Unterricht*, XVI (1965), 695–9.

Honselmann, K. "Die Veröffentlichung der Ablassthesen Martin Luthers 1517," *Theologie und Glaube*, LV (1965), 1–23.

———. *Urfassung und Drucke der Ablassthesen Martin Luthers und ihre Veröffentlichung*. Paderborn: 1966.

Iserloh, E. "Luthers Thesenanschlag, Tatsache oder Legende?" *Trierer theologische Zeitschrift*, LXX (1961), 303–12.

———. *Luthers Thesenanschlag, Tatsache oder Legende?* Wiesbaden: 1962.

———. "Der Thesenanschlag fand nicht statt," *Geschichte in Wissenschaft und Unterricht*, XVI (1965), 675–82.

Kalkoff, P. *Forschungen zu Luthers römischen Prozess*. Rome: 1905.

———. *Ablass und Reliquienverehrung an der Schlosskirche zu Wittenberg unter Friedrich dem Weisen*. Gotha: 1907.

Köhler, W. *Dokumente zum Ablassstreit von 1517*. 2nd ed. Tübingen: 1934.

Körner, F. *Tezel, der Ablassprediger. Sein Leben und sein Wirken für den Ablass seiner Zeit*. Frankenberg: 1880.

Lau, F. "Zweifel um den 31. Oktober 1517?" *Lutherische Monatshefte*, I (1962), 459–63.

Lohse, B. "Der Stand der Debatte über Luthers Thesenanschlag," *Luther*, XXXIV (1963), 132–6.

Luther, J. *Vorbereitung und Verbreitung von M. Luthers 95 Thesen*. Berlin: 1933.

Meinhold, P. "Luthers Thesenanschlag fand doch statt," *Christ und Welt*, XV (August 3, 1962), 10.

Meissinger, K. *Der katholische Luther*. Munich: 1952.

Myconius, F. *Geschichte der Reformation*, ed. O. Clemen. Leipzig: n.d.

Paulus, N. *Johann Tetzel, der Ablassprediger*. Mainz: 1899.

———. *Geschichte des Ablasses im Mittelalter*. 3 vols. Paderborn: 1922–23.

Scheurl, C. *Briefbuch*, ed. Freiherr von Soden and J. K. F. Knaake. Vol. II. Potsdam: 1872; reprinted, Aalen: 1962.

Steitz, H. "Martin Luthers Ablassthesen von 1517. Bericht über die Diskussion, 1957–1965," *Geschichte in Wissenschaft und Unterricht*, XVI (1965), 661–74.

Steubing, H. "Hat Luther die 95 Thesen wirklich angeschlagen?" *Kirche in der Zeit*, XX (1965), 447–52.

Volz, H. *Martin Luthers Thesenanschlag und dessen Vorgeschichte*. Weimar: 1959.

———. "Erzbischof Albrecht von Mainz und Martin Luthers 95 Thesen," *Jahrbuch der Hessischen kirchengeschichtlichen Vereinigung*, XIII (1962), 187–228.

———. "Der Thesenanschlag fand—und zwar wahrscheinlich am 1. November 1517—statt," *Geschichte in Wissenschaft und Unterricht*, XVI (1965), 682–6.

INDEX